BOUNDARIES
WITH KIDS
WORKBOOK

Resources by Henry Cloud and John Townsend

Books

Boundaries (and workbook)
Boundaries in Dating (and workbook)
Boundaries in Marriage (and workbook)
Boundaries with Kids (and workbook)
Boundaries with Teens (Townsend)
Changes That Heal (and workbook) (Cloud)
Hiding from Love (Townsend)
How People Grow (and workbook)
How to Have That Difficult Conversation You've Been Avoiding
Making Small Groups Work
The Mom Factor (and workbook)
Raising Great Kids
Raising Great Kids Workbook for Parents of Preschoolers
Raising Great Kids Workbook for Parents of School-Age Children
Raising Great Kids Workbook for Parents of Teenagers
Safe People (and workbook)
12 "Christian" Beliefs That Can Drive You Crazy

Video Curriculum

Boundaries
Boundaries in Dating
Boundaries in Marriage
Boundaries with Kids
Raising Great Kids for Parents of Preschoolers
ReGroup (with Bill Donahue)

Audio

Boundaries
Boundaries in Dating
Boundaries in Marriage
Boundaries with Kids
Boundaries with Teens (Townsend)
Changes That Heal (Cloud)
How People Grow
How to Have That Difficult Conversation You've Been Avoiding
Making Small Groups Work
The Mom Factor
Raising Great Kids

BOUNDARIES WITH KIDS
WORKBOOK

HOW HEALTHY
CHOICES
GROW HEALTHY
CHILDREN

DR. HENRY CLOUD & DR. JOHN TOWNSEND

WITH LISA GUEST

ZONDERVAN®

ZONDERVAN.com/
AUTHORTRACKER
follow your favorite authors

We want to hear from you. Please send your comments about this book to us in care of zreview@zondervan.com. Thank you.

ZONDERVAN

Boundaries with Kids Workbook
Copyright © 1998 by Henry Cloud and John Townsend

Requests for information should be addressed to:

Zondervan, *Grand Rapids, Michigan 49530*

ISBN 978-0-310-22349-8

Published in association with Yates & Yates, www.yates2.com.

Printed in the United States of America

09 10 11 12 13 14 15 • 48 47 46 45 44 43 42 41 40 39 38 37 36 35 34 33 32 31 30 29 28 27 26 25 24 23

Contents

Part 3: Implementing Boundaries with Kids

Introduction

A wise friend once rightly observed that parenting is relentless. Indeed, the task of helping children develop inside them what you, their parents, have been providing on the outside—responsibility, self-control, and freedom—is not an easy one. But *Boundaries with Kids* can help.

We have organized the book around key concepts that will help children take ownership of their lives. These principles arise from our study of the Bible and God's teaching on responsibility, stewardship, and self-control. We believe these principles of boundaries with children are universal, and they work with kids at all levels of development. In each chapter of the text we included many examples and illustrations of how those laws are applied at all age levels; in this book the application will be more personal.

But keep in mind that *Boundaries with Kids* is geared much more toward how you, the parent, behave with your children than toward educating your children. Learning boundaries has much to do with going through experiences such as receiving consequences for behavior, learning to take ownership, and dealing with the boundaries of others. As you learn to require responsibility from your children, your children learn the value of being responsible. The process begins with you.

You are not in this alone, though. Remember that God is also a parent and has gone through the same pains you are experiencing as you try to teach responsibility to the kids in your life. God understands, and he will guide and help your willing heart (Psalm 1:6). So ask him for his help, wisdom, and resources as you continue the process of helping young people grow up into maturity in him.

HENRY CLOUD, PhD
JOHN TOWNSEND, PhD

Before We Start . . .

- What role(s) do you have in kids' lives?

Parent	Daycare worker
Teacher	Babysitter or nanny
Grandparent	Church youth worker
Coach	Sunday school teacher
Neighbor	

  Or are you a teen working on establishing your own boundaries?

- What do you hope to gain from reading the text and using this workbook? Put differently, which of the following, if any, are currently issues with you and the kid(s) in your life?

Impulsivity	Aggressive behavior
Inattention to parental directives	School problems
Defying authority	Conflicts with friends
Whining	Sexual involvement
Procrastination	Drugs
Inability to finish tasks	Gangs

  Things are going well—and I want to keep it that way!

Part 1

Why Kids
Need Boundaries

Chapter 1

The Future Is Now

- I (Dr. Cloud) was surprised to find Allison cleaning her fourteen-year-old son's room. When I said, "I just feel sorry for Cameron's future wife," Allison straightened up, froze for a moment, and then hurried from the room. After a few moments, she looked at me and said, "I've never thought about it that way."

  — In what ways might you, like Allison, be parenting in the present without thinking about the future?

  — What can you do to keep an eye on the future?

- A person's character is one's destiny. A person's character (his abilities and inabilities, his moral makeup, his functioning in relationships, and how he does tasks) largely determines how he will function in life (whether he does well in love and in work).

  — Look in the mirror. How has your character—your strengths as well as your weaknesses—determined how you have functioned in life? In love? In work?

  — What are some of the character strengths and weaknesses you already see in your children?

- If a person's character makeup determines his future, then child rearing is primarily about helping children to develop character that will take them through life safely, securely, productively, and joyfully. A major goal of raising children is to help them develop the character that will make their future go well.

  — What character traits have served you well in your adult years? What do you remember your parents and other significant adults doing to encourage those traits?

  — Had they been strengthened as you were growing up, what character traits would have benefited you in your adult years? What are you doing to strengthen those traits now?

- What wake-up call does Allison's experience offer you? As you consider your child's future, what element of your parenting (if any) do you now recognize as sowing seeds for character weakness?

The future is now. When you are a parent, you help create a child's future. The patterns children establish early in life (their character) they will live out later. And character is always formed in relationship. We can't overestimate your role in developing this character. As Proverbs says, "Train a child in the way he should go, and when he is old he will not turn from it" (22:6).

Preventive Medicine (page 16)*

- From our own experience and that of our audiences and readers, one thing became obvious to us. Adults with boundary problems had not developed those problems as grownups. They had learned patterns early in life and then continued those out-of-control patterns in their adult lives, where the stakes were higher.

---

*The subtitles and page numbers refer to corresponding sections and pages in the book *Boundaries with Kids*.

— Review the list of boundary problems found on pages 16–17. Which of them, if any, have been problems for you during your adult years?

— What seeds for these out-of-control patterns in your adult life do you see as you look back on your childhood?

• Parents began to ask for this book. They knew the pain they had been through and did not want their children to go through the same kind of learning curve. Basically, they wanted answers to three questions.

  1. How do I teach boundaries to children?
  2. How do I enforce my own boundaries with my children in appropriate ways?
  3. How can I ensure that my children will not have the problems with boundaries that I have had?

— Which of these three questions states your greatest concern?

— What other questions, if any, do you hope to have answered by *Boundaries with Kids*?

We want to help you answer your questions and help your children develop the character that will lead them into the life that God created them to have.

Children Are Not Born with Boundaries (page 17)

A boundary is a "property line" that defines a person; it defines where one person ends and someone else begins. If we know where a person's boundaries are, we know what we can expect this person to take control of: himself or herself. We can require responsibility in regard to feelings, behaviors, and attitudes.

- A child needs to know where she begins, what she needs to take responsibility for, and what she does not need to take responsibility for. If she grows up in relationships where she is confused about her own boundaries (what she is responsible for) and about others' boundaries (what they are responsible for), she does not develop the self-control that will enable her to steer through life successfully.

  — What relationships during your childhood, if any, caused you confusion about your boundaries, and what you were really responsible for?

  — What relationships, if any, in your children's life might be causing them confusion about their boundaries and about what they are really responsible for?

- Children internalize boundaries from external relationships and discipline. In order for children to learn who they are and what they are responsible for, their parents have to have clear boundaries with them and relate to them in ways that help them learn their own boundaries.

  — What might your child be learning about boundaries from their significant external relationships? From the kinds of discipline they receive?

  — How clear are your boundaries? Chapter 3—"Kids Need Parents with Boundaries"—will help, but the *Boundaries* book and workbook would be a great help, too.

When boundaries are clear, children develop a well-defined sense of who they are and what they are responsible for; the ability to choose; the understanding that if they choose well, things will go well and if they choose poorly, they will suffer; and the possibility of true love based in freedom. Self-control, responsibility, freedom, and love—what could be a better outcome of parenting than that?

The Three Roles of a Parent (page 19)

Some people see a parent as a coach, some as a police officer, some as a friend, some as God. In part, all of these roles have some truth to them. In our view, the parent or caretaker role consists of three main functions.

- *Guardian:* A guardian is legally responsible for a child and, in that capacity, protects and preserves the child.

  — When have you been especially conscious of your child's need for protection and preservation? What did you do in response to that need?

  — Balancing freedom and limits becomes a major task in child rearing. What are some boundaries and limits parents could set to protect a child from the following sources of danger?

  Dangers within themselves

  Dangers in the outside world

  Inappropriate freedoms that they are not ready to handle

  Never-appropriate or evil actions, behaviors, or attitudes

  Their own regressive tendency to remain dependent and avoid growing up

More often than not in their role as guardian, parents use boundaries to keep their child safe, growing, and healthy. They set limits to freedom and then enforce them for the child's protection. Through this process, the child internalizes the limits as wisdom and slowly begins to be able to take care of herself.

- *Manager:* A manager makes sure things get done—goals are reached, demands and expectations are met. Children are not born with self-discipline; therefore they have to have "other-discipline."

  — In what child-rearing situation have you functioned as a manager? Give a specific example.

  — Managers provide this "other-discipline" that a child needs by controlling resources, teaching, enforcing consequences, correcting, chastising, maintaining order, and building skills. Which technique(s) did you use, or could you have used, in the example you just gave?

Boundaries play an important role in managing. Setting limits and requiring the children to take ownership (embracing the problem as their own) and responsibility (taking care of what they have embraced) entail a clear understanding of boundaries. We will talk more about this later.

- *Source:* Parents are the source of all good things (material and immaterial) for a child. They are the bridge to the outside world of resources that sustain life. And in both giving and receiving resources, boundaries play an important role.

  — Being the resource for children is fraught with blessing and difficulty. What blessing have you encountered? What difficulty?

— Do you tend to give too easily or to hold resources too tightly? What risk do you run with that tendency? At this point, what do you think you could do to counter that tendency?

In the beginning, parents are the source. They progressively give children the independence to obtain what they need on their own. We will see how boundaries help structure the resources and how they play an important role in parenting.

Learning to Take Responsibility (page 22)

Boundaries facilitate the process of having the child internalize things (feeling the need or motivation to take responsibility for himself, planning for and taking the time to act responsibly, developing the skills necessary to act responsibly) that were external to him. What was once external becomes internal.

- Consider again Cameron and his mom (see the beginning of this section, page 22).

    — Why didn't Cameron feel the need to clean up his room? Why wasn't he motivated to clean up?

    — Why didn't Cameron plan for or take the time to clean up? Why didn't he have the skill to organize his room?

    — In what ways, if at all, are you—like Allison—keeping your child from taking responsibility for himself?

• What kind of boundaries did Allison need to establish for herself in order for her son to develop boundaries that would serve him well?

As you take a stance of good clear boundaries with children, they will have a better chance of gaining the motivation, the need, the skill, and the plan to live a loving, responsible, righteous, and successful life unto God and others. And this is what character is all about.

In the next chapter we will take a closer look at the kind of character we want to develop in our children.

Chapter 2

What Does Character Look Like?

Like Allison, we want our children to be responsible. But often we don't have a very clear picture of the character we are trying to build. In this chapter we would like to give you some qualities we consider important to adult functioning, qualities in which boundaries play an essential developing role.

Loving (page 23)

Of the three great virtues—faith, hope, and love—the apostle Paul wrote that "the greatest of these is love" (1 Corinthians 13:13). Most parents would say that they want their children to be loving.

- A lack of boundaries can lead to egocentrism, impulse problems, addictions, or irresponsibility.

  — What impact does each of these have on a person's ability to love? Consider . . . Susan, who thinks only of herself: *egocentrism*

    The alcoholic: *addictions and impulse problems*

    George's inability to hold a job: *irresponsibility*

  — Explain "love without the fruits of love is really not love in the end."

- Loving people respect the boundaries of others.

  — When has someone's failure to respect your boundaries made his or her love not feel very much like love?

  — In what ways, if at all, are your weak or nonexistent boundaries interfering with your ability to be loving?

  — What are you doing, or could be doing, to teach your children to be more loving, to be more respectful of people's boundaries?

Responsible (page 25)

Being responsible means taking ownership of your life. Ownership is to truly possess your life and to know that you are accountable for your life—to God and others. Responsibility therefore includes such things as duty or obligations, reliability and dependability, and just "getting the job done."

- Our boundaries define and protect our feelings, attitudes, behaviors, choices, limits, talents, thoughts, desires, values, and loves—and truly responsible people take ownership of these things. A responsible person says, "My feelings are *my* problem" or "My attitude is *my* problem" or, unlike Adam and Eve in the Garden, "*I* made me do it." With this understanding and ownership, self-control can develop.

  — When have you recently hesitated to take responsibility for your feelings, attitudes, behaviors, choices, limits, talents, thoughts, desires, values, or loves? What kept you from doing so?

— When have you recently seen your child hesitate or even fail to take responsibility for her feelings, attitudes, behaviors, choices, limits, talents, thoughts, desires, values, or loves? Why did she hesitate? How did you respond—or how would you have liked to respond?

• We shall all give an account to God for our lives (2 Corinthians 5:10), and he will hold us responsible for what we did with our talents, resources, relationships, time, and actions.

— What are you doing with the life that has been entrusted to you? Put differently, how would this accounting go if you came face to face with God today?

— What boundary problems, if any, are interfering with what you are doing with your life?

Free (page 27)

Victims feel as if they have no choices in life. Life is something that happens to them, and whatever comes their way is their lot.

• Remember the woman with the talkative coworker? Remember Joe, whose company was imposing some new work policies? When, if ever, have you—like these two—suddenly realized that you could act rather than remain passive in a situation, that you had choices and could take greater control of your life? Explain the course of action you took and how you benefited.

- Children raised with good boundaries learn that they are not only responsible for their lives, but also free to live their lives any way they choose—as long as they take responsibility for their choices.

  — What do you see around you that supports the assertion that "we live in a society of victims"? Be specific.

  — In what areas of your life, if at all, are you living more as a victim than a free and responsible adult?

  — In what areas of your child's life, if at all, are you letting him claim to be a victim rather than encouraging him to be responsible for what is happening in his life? Consider, for instance, his friendships, school situations, and involvement in sports.

Initiating (page 29)

A normal part of human behavior is to initiate things. Being created in the image of God is being created with the ability to begin something.

- Often a problem with initiating things is a boundary problem.

  — Is there a Dave in your life—in your relationships or your workplace? Or are you a Dave? In what areas of your life, if at all, are you failing to take initiative?

  — What kinds of boundary problems contribute to the failure to take initiative? Review the definition of boundaries under "Responsible."

- A child needs to be required to initiate, an important aspect of boundary training.

  — What, if anything, kept you from learning that "you are responsible for your own fun"? When did you learn that fact about life?

  — What are you doing, or could you be doing, to teach your child that he is "responsible for his own fun"?

Respectful of Reality (page 30)

The character that creates a life that works must have a healthy respect for reality. By reality we mean experiencing the consequences of our actions in the real world.

- Every person has to come to the realization that one's actions have real consequences in a real world.

  — When did you learn that your actions have real consequences in a real world? Did the positive side of consequences (rewards for hard work) or the negative side (the costs of goofing off) contribute more to your learning?

  — What, if anything, interfered when you were learning this lesson? Did someone, for instance, bail you out so you didn't have to deal with the consequences of your actions? Were you allowed to think that the consequences of your actions were meant for someone else?

- Mature adults have a healthy respect for reality. They know that, for the most part, if they do good, good things will happen. If they do nothing or do bad, bad things will happen. This dual respect for the positive and negative sides of reality is often referred to as wisdom.

  — What are you doing, or could be doing, to teach your child that accomplishment comes one day at a time?

  — What are you doing, or could be doing, to teach your child that goofing off and laziness will cost her?

Growing (page 31)

Few things inspire us like a story of a person's growing and overcoming some difficult obstacle, especially in her own character. The ability to grow is a character issue.

- Good parenting can help a child develop character that faces the obstacles of life with an orientation toward growth. It includes developing abilities and gaining knowledge as well as facing negative things about oneself that need changing.

  — This section opens with examples of growth—of growing in difficult situations and of growing in normal circumstances. What example of personal growth are you most proud of? What factors contributed to that growth?

  — Review the list of character qualities that enable growth (page 32). Which of these, if any, have you struggled with or do you continue to struggle with?

— Which of these character qualities does your child especially need to work on? What might you do to help her?

- Boundaries help children see what is expected of them and how they need to grow to meet those expectations. Parents need to require their children to do the changing, instead of trying to get reality to change.

    — Consider carefully this perspective on your role in your child's life. How might it influence your parenting when your child bumps up against a family rule or a school rule?

    — When has failure to change cost you? Practice telling that story in terms your child can understand and plan to share your experience with her when appropriate.

Oriented to Truth (page 34)

A less-than-honest person is somewhere between a pain and a catastrophe. Dishonesty fuels betrayal, blocks intimacy, and prevents growth. To the extent that a person is able and willing to be honest, he can grow.

- Honesty begins with parents who model it, require it from their children, and provide them with a safe environment in which to be honest.

    — What did your parents do to teach honesty or the importance of being honest? What did they say? What did they model?

— What were the consequences—logical or relational—when you failed to be honest?

— When, if ever, have you struggled to be honest? What did you fear (anger, shame, guilt, condemnation, or abandonment) that tempted you to lie?

- Boundaries require the truth, and boundaries give the safety of known consequences for failure. Children can handle the known logical consequences of their mistakes much better than they can handle relational consequences such as anger, guilt, shame, condemnation, or abandonment.

  — What are you teaching your child about honesty through your words? Your actions?

  — What logical consequences have you established—or would you like to establish—for those times when your child is less than honest?

Oriented to Transcendence (page 35)

The most important questions that anyone has to answer are "Who is God?" and "Is it me, or is it God?" The answers govern every direction of a person's life.

- Being grounded in God gives direction and meaning to human existence, allowing people to transcend life, problems, their own limitations and mistakes, and other people's sins against them. Without an orientation to transcend the realities of this life and touch the realities of God, people are very limited.

— What did your parents do to orient you to transcendence and help you wrestle with the questions "Who is God?" and "Is it me, or is it God?" What did your parents say? What did they model? What freedom did they give you in your struggle to define and perhaps even take ownership of a relationship with God?

— When has your orientation to transcendence helped you deal with life's harsh realities? Be specific about the circumstances and how being grounded in God (to whatever degree) helped you through.

• People who have the ability to transcend themselves go beyond their own existence to the reality of others, God, and virtues they hold more important than themselves and their own immediate happiness. In short, because they realize that life is bigger than they are, they become bigger than they are at any given moment to meet its demands. Humility makes them larger than they were.

— What are you saying and doing to orient your child to transcendence? What would you like to do in this regard?

— When, if at all, has your child's or your family's grounding in God helped your child face a crisis or struggle? Be specific about the circumstances and how being grounded in God (to whatever degree) helped your child through.

A Tall Order (page 36)

Seeing character building as a task of parenting can be overwhelming. It is certainly easier to manage the moment or to do what comes naturally. But the need is greater and higher. As we said before, a child's character will determine much of the course his life takes.

- In *The Seven Habits of Highly Effective People*, author Stephen Covey says, "Begin with the end in mind." Summarize "the end" you have in mind as you think about the adult you want your child to become. Describe that person.

- What was the most challenging aspect of this chapter for you? The most encouraging?

To develop a child of good character, we have to be parents of good character. As the questions in this chapter have suggested, to develop boundaries in our children, *we* have to have boundaries. And that's the subject of the next chapter.

Chapter 3

Kids Need Parents with Boundaries

"Problem kids" like Wayne don't evolve in a vacuum. Every problem child generally has a problem context, and kids with healthy limits don't grow them out of thin air. Although by nature we resist limits from birth, we have a lot of help either developing boundaries or not developing them.

- Whenever you begin to look at where boundary conflicts and development problems come from, "look to the rock from which you were cut and to the quarry from which you were hewn" (Isaiah 51:1).

  — Were you a problem child like Wayne—disruptive, pushy, intrusive, and sassy with adults? Or were you at the opposite end of the spectrum or somewhere in between?

  — Consider for a moment "the rock from which you were cut." What kind of help did you have at home either developing or not developing boundaries? In what ways did you respond—either defensively or responsibly—to the parenting you received in regard to boundaries? Give specific examples.

— Now look at the quarry from which your child is hewn. What kind of help has she had so far either developing or not developing boundaries? In what ways is she responding—either defensively or responsibly—to the parenting you are offering in regard to boundaries?

• Neither the religious world that blames problems on a child and his sinful nature nor the counseling world that blames out-of-control children on what happened to them as they were growing up is completely accurate. Instead, who we are today is essentially the result of two forces: our environment and our responses to it.

— Why is this statement both good news and bad news?

Our parenting, significant relationships, and circumstances powerfully shape our character and attitudes. But how we react to our significant relationships and circumstances—whether defensively or responsibly—also influences what kind of person we become. A parent with boundaries is therefore the first and most important ingredient in helping children learn boundaries.

Your Child Is Reacting to Your Parenting (page 39)

Wayne had problems; the problems were Wayne's and he needed to work on them. But another principle is at work here: *We need to interpret our child's behavior as a response to our own* rather than looking at his actions in terms of his motives, needs, personality, and circumstances.

• Wayne may indeed be impulsive, self-centered, or immature, but consider his parents for a moment.

— In what ways was Wayne responding to his mom's style of relating to him? His dad's?

- As a rule, children don't know what they are doing. They have little idea how to handle life so that it works right. That's why God gave them parents—to love them, give them structure, and guide them into maturity. Basically, children will mature to the level the parent structures them, and no higher.

  — In general, what picture of the universe did you learn at home? What did you learn about reality, love, freedom, and choices? What specifically did you learn about responsibility and the consequences of irresponsibility?

  — What is your child learning, from your style of relating, about reality, love, freedom, and choices? What specifically is he learning, from your parenting, about responsibility and the consequences of irresponsibility?

  — When you see your child misbehave, why is it helpful to ask yourself, "What was my part in creating this problem?"

Looking at the plank in your eye rather than the speck of sawdust in your child's (see Matthew 7:1-5) may be painful, but it will help you recognize the work you need to do on yourself. We suggest you pick up a copy of the *Boundaries* book and workbook if you haven't already read them. (A video curriculum is also available.) Repairing and developing boundaries with God and with the other growing people in your life will help you develop a child with boundaries.

Your Three Avenues of Influence (page 41)

There are three ways you can influence your kids to develop boundaries.

- ***Teaching:*** You can teach your children boundaries—the ability to hear and say no appropriately—just as you teach them to tie their shoes, ride a bike, and clean their rooms. The concepts and principles of boundaries are explicit and clear. They aren't vague, esoteric ideas; instead, they are grounded in reality, God's laws, and everyday life. As a result, you can directly teach boundaries, and your children can learn them.

— In what recent teaching situation could you have used the word *boundary?* Why would that have been helpful?

— Review the age-appropriate teachings outlined on pages 42–43. What guidance do you find here for teaching your child about boundaries?

— Freedom comes from handling responsibility well; it is not a gift bequeathed by chronological age. Why is this principle important especially for young people standing at the threshold of adulthood?

- *Modeling:* Children learn about boundaries from how you operate in your own world. They watch how you treat them, your spouse, and your work. And they emulate you, for good or for bad. In this sense, boundaries are "caught" more than they are "taught."

— In what areas of your life do your efforts to live out healthy boundaries need to be more consistent with what you are trying to teach your child about boundaries? Your spouse may be able to help you answer this.

— Remember Jeremy and the way his mom interrupted him? How would you like to respond when your child points out that you broke a universal rule?

— A child's need to belong is more central than his need to be good. Why? What does this suggest as to how boundaries are modeled and enforced in your home? How can you use boundaries to provide your child with a sense of belonging?

• ***Helping Your Child to Internalize:*** To internalize something is to make it part of yourself. It is making a fact an experienced reality. If your boundary training consists only of words, you are wasting your breath. But if you "do" boundaries with your kids, they internalize the experiences, remember them, digest them, and make them part of how they see reality.

— When they experienced parental boundaries, Ricky and Benny learned a lesson in fiscal responsibility and began to internalize the reality that if you spend it now, you won't have it later. As a kid, what lesson did you experience as a reality and therefore learn?

— For a child to develop boundaries, a parent with boundaries needs to stand like an oak tree that a child runs her head into over and over again until she realizes that the tree is stronger than she is and walks around it next time. In what areas of parenting are you standing strong like an oak? What lessons is that helping your children learn? In what areas do you need to strengthen your boundaries so you can stand stronger?

Obstacles to Teaching Boundaries (page 45)

Teaching boundaries is difficult! Part of the challenge is tolerating and enduring your child's hatred of your boundaries. The kid's job is to test your resolve so she can learn about reality. Your job is to withstand the test, including anger, pouting, tantrums, and much more. No wonder most parents struggle to maintain boundaries and train their children to develop them! Below are a few obstacles to be aware of.

- *Depending on the Child:* There is no greater ingredient of growth for your young-ster than love. As your child's major source of love, you provide the closeness, inti-macy, and nurture that sustains her. Yet this closeness can become confused with a parent's need for the child. This is called dependency. It is the reverse of what the parenting relationship should be.

  — Why is it a problem for the parent as well as the child when a parent needs a child's closeness or affection to meet his or her own unmet needs?

  — Where in the dance between Beverly and Samantha (if at all) do you see your-self as parent or child?

  — Are you afraid that if you say no to your kids, you will lose the love you need from them? To help you answer that tough question, consider where you are getting the love you need (Genesis 2:18) or where you could be getting it.

- *Overidentifying with the Child:* Parents need to empathize with their children's pain, fear, and loneliness. But some parents confuse their own painful feelings with their child's and project their problems onto the child. What might be discomfort for the toddler is seen as trauma by the mother; what may be anxiety for the teenager is experienced as panic by the father.

— What is the difference between *hurt* and *harm*? Why is this distinction important in parenting?

— What about the Catherine and Gavin scenario do you find helpful?

— If you find that you can't bear your child's pain, you may be projecting your pain into him. What past issues that have not fully healed may be causing you to overidentify with your child? What will you do to resolve those issues?

• ***Thinking Love and Separateness Are Enemies:*** Many parents fear that disagreeing, confronting, or simply being different from their children indicates a break in the connection. But structuring and being separate from your child are not the same thing as a loss of love. The reality is that love and separateness go together and one doesn't threaten the other.

— Explain the statement "You can't really love someone with whom you can't be separate. That is, love does not mean losing yourself, but rather frees you and empowers you to be yourself." What bearing does this statement have on parenting?

— What about yourself, if anything, do you see in how Keith related to Ron? What, if at all, do you need to do with your child that Keith wasn't able to do with Ron? Spell out what your child's choices are going to cost him so that he can begin to mature.

— If you feel that when you tell the truth to your child, love is gone, begin working on being a truthful, honest person with God and the supportive people in your life. What keeps you from being honest? Share those fears honestly with God. With whom can you practice being open and truthful?

- *Ignoring and Zapping:* Ignoring and zapping teaches the child she should persist in whatever she wants. She learns she can "get away with murder" nine times out of ten, and she just needs to learn how to endure the out-of-control parent that one time out of ten.

  — Why is ignoring an unhelpful approach to a child's inappropriate behavior? What harm can zapping cause? Why is consistency in confronting problem behaviors early on important preparation for real life?

  — What did you learn (perhaps about yourself) from Carol's experience with Tess?

  — What aspect of your child's behavior, if any, are you ignoring but resenting, moving closer to the boiling point? Put another way, what aspect of your child's behavior do you need to confront even if it's not especially early in the game? What will you say when you do confront her?

- Being Worn Down: Kids work us and work us and work us. It is scary how they can sense when we are weak and ready to give in to them. Take a moment to consider why your child may be wearing you down.

— Parenting is a temporary (albeit sometimes consuming) job, not an identity. Who are you apart from a parent? What other interests do you have? What other activities do you or could you pursue?

— Kids with parents who have a life learn both that they aren't the center of the universe and that they can be free to pursue their own dreams. What are you teaching your kids from the relationships you maintain and the things you do to fill your tank?

— Who are your cheerleader friends who can help you hold the limits you have set for your child—or where might you find such friends?

Remember, you can't teach what you don't have. Don't just *say* boundaries to your child. *Be* boundaries. If you aren't yet, get to work on yourself. It will pay off for both you and him.

We hope that you have seen the importance of training children in boundaries and of being a parent with boundaries. In the next section you will gain an understanding of the ten laws of boundaries. These guiding principles will help you apply boundaries to many aspects of home life with your kids. Use them as tools to employ and teach responsibility to your children.

Part 2

Ten Boundary Principles
Kids Need to Know

Chapter 4

What Will Happen If I Do This?

The Law of Sowing and Reaping

- Remember Sally's plans for a family day at Disneyland and Susan's plans for shopping with her girls?

  — What did Susan do effectively that Sally didn't?

  — How do Susan's kids benefit from her willingness and ability to identify and enforce consequences? What do they learn?

  — Are you more like Sally or Susan in your follow-through? If you're more like Sally, what do you think keeps you from being more like Susan?

Teaching the Reality Principle (page 58)

Parents run into a big problem when they do not distinguish between relational consequences and reality consequences.

- Life works on reality consequences. Relational consequences usually do not motivate people to change. True change usually comes only when someone's behavior

41

causes him to encounter reality consequences like pain or losses of time, money, possessions, things he enjoys, and people he values.

— When, if ever, have psychological and negative relational consequences motivated you (as a child or adult) to change? How did you tend to react to such consequences as anger, guilt messages, nagging, and love being withdrawn?

— When we are allowed to pay for our mistakes, we learn from them. When have reality consequences prompted you to change? Be specific about the change as well as the prompting.

— Which kind of consequences do you as a parent tend most to rely on in your attempts to have your children cooperate and obey? Why?

• The Law of Sowing and Reaping is a law that we depend on daily, both positively and negatively. God has wired it into the universe, and we can build a life around it.

— The positive side of the Law of Sowing and Reaping gives us a reasonable sense of power and control over our lives. In what are you investing your talents and your life in order to reap good fruit according to this law?

— What healthy fear of bad things does the negative side of the Law of Sowing and Reaping give you?

If our kids never learn the Law of Sowing and Reaping, they lose on both the positive and negative sides of life. They will not have the motivation to do good work and be diligent, and at the same time they will not fear laziness, irresponsibility, and other character problems. Both conditions result in suffering: the loss of good realities and the encountering of bad ones.

Too Bad for Whom? (page 61)

Consequences transfer the need to be responsible from the parent to the child. Consequences make it the child's problem.

- Too many times, children's behavior does not become a problem for them. It doesn't cost them things they value. Instead, parents allow the problem to become a problem for them.

  — Why do parents often fail to let a child's behavior become that child's problem?

  — What could a parent do to overcome the obstacles to teaching consequences that you just identified?

- Think back over the last week or two.

  — In what situation with your child did you carry the worry, strain, and effort rather than letting the problem be his?

  — To figure out what to do next time, consider what you did to keep him from experiencing the problem as his own. What could you do to help him experience the problem as his?

Consequences teach a child "too bad for me." They help him realize "my behavior becomes a problem for *me*." Parents need to help this lesson be learned.

Age and Content Change, the Law Remains the Same (page 62)

The Law of Sowing and Reaping teaches children "self-control" (Galatians 5:23). They learn, "I am in control of the quality of my life." They realize they have a choice whether they are inside and miserable or outside and playing.

- The formula for the Law of Sowing and Reaping is to give children freedom, allow choices, and then manage the consequences accordingly. Heap on praise and increase the freedoms when children use responsibility well.

  — Consider the ages of your kids. What choices does each face regularly? In each situation, what are some appropriate consequences for them to have to manage if they make a poor choice?

  — What additional privileges could result from your kids' good choices?

- When children make bad choices, empathize with their loss. Avoid the "I told you sos."

  — What does empathy do for your relationship with your child that "I told you so" doesn't?

  — Empathy may not come easily to you as a parent, so practice saying aloud statements that reflect empathy rather than blame. Start with the examples on page 63 of the book. Add any that seem more natural to you and that, knowing your kids, you can anticipate having the opportunity to use.

The particulars will change through life, but the Law of Sowing and Reaping is the same: If I make good choices, life is better than if I don't.

Balancing Freedom, Choices, and Consequences (page 63)

The goal of parenting is not to control the child into doing what you want, to "make them." The goal is to give them the choice to do what they want and make it so painful to do the wrong thing that they will not want to. You are letting them choose, but making the Law of Sowing and Reaping have reality.

- Wanting things to go well and wanting to do things our way are not compatible wishes for child or adult.

  — In what recent parenting situation have you, like Joey's mom, had to make sure that your child did not do things her way in order for things to go well for her in the long-term?

  — Parents are in control of the reaping. What benefits do—or could—your children reap when they make good choices? What pain do—or could—they reap when they make poor choices? Give two or three examples of both benefits and pain.

- Parenting means giving freedom, requiring responsibility, rendering consequences, and being loving throughout. And freedom, responsibility, consequences, and love must all be held in balance.

  — Why doesn't self-control exist without freedom and choices?

  — Why do you think a balance of freedom, responsibility, and consequences results in a person's being loving and doing the right things for the right reasons?

Children need to learn by experience that if they sow to irresponsibility, they will reap pain, and if they sow to responsible behavior, they will reap the benefits and want to choose that path.

Running Interference (page 65)

Parents have difficulty allowing their children to suffer consequences. The natural tendency is to bail them out.

- Remember the child who, late at night, needed glue for a school project due the next morning?

  — What was your initial reaction to Mom number one? To Mom number two?

  — What, if anything, keeps you from regularly being a Mom number two? What are you afraid of? Why do you interrupt consequences before they teach your child a lesson for life?

- Parents need to be comfortable with letting the child suffer. As the Bible says, "No discipline seems pleasant at the time, but painful. Later on, however, it produces a harvest of righteousness and peace for those who have been trained by it" (Hebrews 12:11).

  — Were your parents comfortable letting you suffer? Explain your answer.

  — Suffering the consequences of poor choices is inevitable in life. Why is it better to do that suffering earlier instead of later?

If you find it difficult to allow your child to suffer consequences, be sure to find someone to help you through your own resistance.

Balancing Grace and Truth (page 67)

In short, the recipe for a growing person is always grace plus truth over time. Give a person grace (unmerited favor) and truth (structure) and do that over time, and you have the greatest chance of this person growing into a person of good character.

- Grace includes support, resources, love, compassion, forgiveness, and all of the relational sides of God's nature.

  — What aspects of grace did you receive growing up?

  — What forms of grace are you offering to your kids?

- Truth is the structure of life; it tells us how we are supposed to live our lives and how life really works.

  — What truths structure life for your kids?

  — Are these truths more than just conceptual for your kids? Offer supporting evidence for your answer.

If Mom tells her child that it's good for him to do *a*, *b*, or *c*, then he needs for that to be reality for him to learn it. It is her job to make it real. Then and only then is the truth *really* true.

Making Good the Law of Sowing and Reaping (page 68)

The list of reality consequences is endless. The only end is your own creativity. Consider again these principles for determining reality consequences.

- Make the consequences a natural outflow of the crime.

    — Why are natural or logical consequences effective?

    — In what recent or recurring parenting situation could you incorporate natural consequences to teach the Law of Sowing and Reaping?

- Save consequences for serious offenses in which the behavior may become a bad character pattern.

    — Why is this strategy wise?

    — What "serious offenses" warrant consequences in your home?

- Give immediate consequences.

    — Why is immediacy important?

    — What keeps parents from responding immediately?

- Stay away from emotional consequences, and effect reality consequences.
  — Why is it wise to avoid strictly emotional consequences?

  — What benefits—long-term as well as short-term—come with reality consequences?

- Use relational consequences only if they concern your own feelings.
  — Why do parents need to be careful of using relational consequences?

  — In what kind of situation in your home would relational consequences be logical or natural? Be specific.

- Think of consequences as protecting yourself and the rest of the family from the behavior of the child.
  — Why is this perspective helpful?

  — In what parenting situation would letting consequences happen have benefited your family as well as helped the guilty party learn the Law of Sowing and Reaping?

- Preserve choice as much as possible.
  — Why is it important to preserve a child's choice as much as possible?

  — Why is preserving a child's choice difficult?

- Make sure there is not a good reason a child is misbehaving before invoking consequences.
  — When, if ever, have you regretted not doing this?

  — What are some "good reasons" parents need to be alert for?

- Talk to the child and ask about the misbehavior when the child is not misbehaving.
  — Why is this a good idea?

  — When have you learned something important by talking with your child's misbehavior when she is not misbehaving?

A Further Word on Rewards and Consequences (page 70)

We believe in rewards for acquiring new skills and performing exceptionally.

- We do not believe in rewards for doing the age-appropriate requirements of civilized people (such as living skills) and doing what is expected (such as work).

  — Do you agree with us about the appropriate use of rewards? Why or why not?

  — How, if at all, will this discussion impact your parenting? What about your use of rewards, if anything, will you change as a result of this discussion?

- A mom told me recently that she had told her son to do something minimal and his reply was "What will you give me?" She asked me what a good reward would be. I told her to tell him that she would give him a very hard time if he didn't do what she asked.

  — Look around at the world today. In what situations that you're aware of are rewards given out too easily?

  — Why is the liberal bestowal of rewards unwise? What does it teach?

We caution you to be careful of giving children the attitude that they only have to perform when someone pays them for it. They need to learn that they will have to pay if they don't perform.

Reality as Friend (page 72)

Maturity is when we stop demanding that life meet our demands and begin to meet the demands of life. The Law of Sowing and Reaping forces us to meet the demands of life, or we experience pain.

- Why is reality not our enemy, but our friend?

- Summarize what you have learned from this chapter about using reality for your children's benefit and growth.

Do your children a favor and teach them to make friends with reality early in life. It is cheaper and safer (and your dinners will begin on time). To make friends with reality, your children must learn to be responsible for the right things. In the next chapter, we will show you what those things are.

Chapter 5

Pulling My Own Wagon

The Law of Responsibility

- When Mom and Dad stopped arbitrating their arguments, Ricky and Benny began learning a valuable boundary lesson: They are responsible for themselves and their struggles. *Children need to know that their problems are their own problems, no one else's.* Their life is their own little red wagon, and their job is to pull it without expecting someone else to.

  — Can you identify a situation when you tried to find someone to blame or to solve a problem for you rather than trying to solve that problem yourself?

  — Why do we human beings often hesitate to solve our problems ourselves?

  — In what current or recurring situation do you see your children trying to find someone to blame or solve a problem for them rather than trying to solve that problem themselves? What kind of coaching can you offer them?

A large part of your boundary training with your kids will have to do with helping them understand that they must gradually take responsibility for their own problems. What begins as the parent's burden must end up as the child's. That is because mature adults see themselves as problem solvers. Immature people experience life as victims and constantly want someone else to solve their problems.

- These are difficult words for many people, especially adults who have been hurt in their childhood and find themselves having to repair what was broken rather than whoever caused the problem.

  — What brokenness from childhood, if any, are you responsible for repairing even though you didn't cause the problem?

  — God's solution to these unfair situations of life is for us to grieve, forgive, and grow through them. What is keeping you from doing so, or, if you have begun this journey, what kind of hope and healing are you finding? In either case, be specific as you answer the question.

Even though we have all been sinned against and mistreated in some ways, our own responses to our environment are the major determining forces in our present character and personality. The child bears most of the weight of his own development.

What Kids Need to Take Responsibility For (page 76)

The aspects of life for which your kids need to take responsibility we call their *treasures*, or things of great value. Part of that treasure is our character—how we love, work, and serve. Let's look at some of the treasures for which your child needs to take ownership.

- *Emotions:* Like all of us, Nathan needed to use feelings in the ways for which God created them: as signals about the state of our soul. Nathan, for instance, needed to identify the source of his anger and solve whatever problem in life had led up to it.

— Which emotions, if any, do you personally have trouble taking ownership of or controlling in a healthy way? What will you do to resolve this and thereby improve what you are modeling for your children?

— Which emotions do your kids seem to have particular difficulty managing? What might you do to help them? For some ideas, look again at Cheryl's words to Nathan (see page 76).

Just as Nathan did, your kids can become the master of their emotions. They can learn to feel their emotions but not let the emotion carry them out of control. That ability is what it means for a child to own one of his treasures: his feelings.

• *Attitudes:* Attitudes are the stances or opinions we take toward people and issues. Children need to see that attitudes are something they work out and decide for themselves and that others' attitudes may not be the same as theirs. We need to help them see the consequences of their attitudes, how they need to take responsibility for them.

— What attitudes do you see each of your children taking toward the following?

Self (strengths and weaknesses, likes and dislikes)

Role in the family

Friends

God (who he is and how to relate to him)

School (their interests and duties)

Work

Moral issues (sex, drugs, gangs)

What red flags, if any, do you see in your answers? What will you do about those attitudes?

— Remember Jesus' Log and Speck principle (Matthew 7:1–5)? When kids have a problem, they (like adults) need first to examine what they may have done to contribute to the problem. What will you do to teach or reinforce this principle in your home this week? (The chart on page 78 offers some questions parents can use to help kids recognize the log in their eye.)

You will do your kids immeasurable favors by helping them experience the reality of Jesus' Log and Speck principle and teaching them to take responsibility for their attitudes.

- **Behavior:** Children learn to conduct themselves in private and in public through love, teaching, modeling, and experiences. They need to learn that how they act is their responsibility.

    — As "impulse disorders," children link their emotions to their actions with no intervening agents such as thoughts, values, or empathy for others. There is a direct line between their feelings and behavior. They have no sense of "what might happen if I act on my feelings?" What have you seen in your children that supports this assertion? Give one or two examples.

— As a parent, you need to make it more painful for your child to be impulsive than to restrain behaviors. You build intervening agents into children by validation, instruction, and experience. In what current situation in your home can you apply these three steps? Plan your strategy below.

Validation

Instruction

Experience

Children don't have to act out feelings. They can express, reflect, symbolize, or delay gratification. Children can learn that they can't always control how they react emotionally, but they can control how they respond behaviorally.

What Kids Need to Understand (page 81)

An understanding of the following two concepts can help ease the pain that comes with being a kid.

- *"It's Hard" vs. "I Can't"*: Another aspect of learning to take responsibility for oneself is for the child to understand that *being unable* differs from *being uncomfortable*. Kids see the two as one. Therefore, what they don't enjoy, they think they can't do. So, since they can't do something they are uncomfortable doing, someone else needs to do it. And that someone else is the boundaryless parent.

— When have you seen your child conclude that being uncomfortable means being unable? What task or action was it that made her uncomfortable?

— What, if anything, did you do in response to her "I can't" conclusion? What would you do differently in a similar situation next time? Remember the dance with Benny and the fact that you are modeling boundaries for your kids.

• Part of growing up is learning what we are responsible for and what we need the help of others on. According to the teaching of Galatians 6, we should bear for one another the overwhelming "boulders"(burdens) in life, but we need to carry our own "knapsacks" (loads). Knapsacks are the normal responsibilities of working, going to school, and fulfilling duties to our friends, family, and church.

— What attitudes do you have toward these knapsacks?

— What attitudes do your kids have toward these knapsacks?

• Kids often see their knapsacks as boulders and want us to solve their problems for them. We need to frustrate this desire and build within them a sense that, while they are to ask for help in matters beyond them (transportation, opportunities to make money, crises), they are expected to handle many things on their own (grades, behavior, tasks).

— What are your kids asking for help with these days—boulders or knapsacks? How are you responding to their requests?

— What are you doing to teach your kids that it's okay to ask for help and that none of us can live life alone?

• Consider the items on the list of a child's jobs when she is dealing with a boulder (see page 83).

Being honest and humble enough to realize you have a problem instead of being proud or denying the problem

Taking the initiative to ask for help from others instead of withdrawing or hoping it will go away

Picking trustworthy people of character you can ask for help

Doing your part to solve the problem

Valuing and appreciating the help that's given

Learning from the experiences so that you don't repeat them

— What are your children learning about these jobs from your modeling?

— In what areas have you seen your kids demonstrate that they are tackling these tasks?

— What will you do to help them with the other tasks?

This is the bad news in life: Even when we are unable to help ourselves, we still have a job to do. If you are hit by a car, you're a victim—but you still have to hobble to the physical therapist and do the exercises. If your best friend moves away, it's not your fault—but it's your job to find other people of character in whom to entrust your heart. There are very few "boulders" in life in which the child has no responsibility at all.

- ***Loving vs. Rescuing:*** Learning the difference between help and rescue is one of the most important lessons in your child's course on responsibility. He is responsible *for* himself. He is responsible *to* others. He is to care about his family and friends and go out of his way to help them. But responsibility dictates that he refrain from protecting them from the consequences of their own actions.

    — Identify some moments when your child has acted with enormous self-centeredness and some moments when she has offered her friends incredible caretaking.

    — When, if ever, have you seen your child act as if she is responsible *for* her friends and not just to them?

- Children don't learn about loving and rescuing from a book. Kids learn about loving and rescuing at home.

  — What did you learn about loving and rescuing in the home where you grew up?

  — What are your children learning from you? How, for instance, do you handle a bad day? How do you tend to handle their skinned knees?

- Kids need to withstand the intense social pressure not to tell about a friend who is into drugs or cheats on exams. They also need to learn how to say no to their friends' demands to solve their problems, take care of their feelings, and make them happy. A major reason children rescue is that they have learned it's the only way to keep a friend.

  — What can you do to help your child choose better friends?

  — When have you seen your child disagree with a friend? Why is this a good sign?

- It's easy to slip into allowing a child to rescue and become confused about responsibility.

  — When, if ever, have you seen someone parent a parent? How did that role affect that person's other relationships?

— In what ways, if at all, are you letting your children parent you? What needs, if any, are you inappropriately looking to your child to meet? Who is a better person to turn to—or where could you find a healthy, safe friend?

Don't burden your children with your hurts. Your child has enough work to do in growing up. At the same time, learn the balance between helping him not to rescue and how to attend to the genuine needs of his family and friends. Learning to love begins with first receiving empathy, then understanding our duty to respect and care for others.

How can a child who is so small and weak have so much power over a grownup? The next law of boundaries deals with this issue: helping your child own the real power he has and give up the power he shouldn't have.

— *Chapter 6* —

I Can't Do It All, But I'm Not Helpless, Either

The Law of Power

I (Dr. Townsend) remember quite clearly the moment when, under the influence of *Tom Sawyer*, I returned home after running away for a few hours, very aware that I was wanting to be powerful and independent, yet faced with my own powerlessness.

Power and Children (page 87)

At some time or another, children think they are grown up, strong, and without limitations. Then, if parents don't get in God's way, kids run into the reality that they don't have as much power as they thought. They have to make some adjustments to life, and they grow from the experience. They adapt to reality rather than demanding that reality adapt to them.

- To develop appropriate boundaries, children need to have power, or *the ability to control something*. Power can range from putting a puzzle together to dancing in a recital, from solving a conflict to developing a successful friendship.

    — In what areas does each of your children enjoy a certain amount of power?

    — What do your children do when they face something they can't control?

- An infant and her parents illustrate the paradox of kids and power.

  — Why would an infant argue that she has no power?

  — What specific evidence would her parents use to argue that she does indeed exert power in the family?

Children's survival and growth in the world depend on an appropriate, reality-based appraisal of the following: what they do and don't have power over, the extent of their power over the things they do control, and how they adapt to the things they can't control.

Power, Powerlessness, and Boundaries (page 88)

Learning the proper use of power helps children develop their boundaries. Mature people know what they have power over and what they don't. Your child needs to learn what he has power over, what he doesn't have power over, and how to tell the difference (to paraphrase the Serenity Prayer).

- A child is forever attempting to have power over things that aren't his. But *he can't set boundaries around that which isn't his property*. When he tries, the real owner will eventually tear down his fences.

  — When have you seen your child encounter this truth? Consider, for instance, a time when he tried to bully a friend. What happened?

  — Why are such times helpful lessons about omnipotence?

- The second problem the child faces is that, *in trying to control the uncontrollable, he negates his ability to exercise power over what he does have.* He is so focused on the first that he neglects the second.

  — What will a child be neglecting if he is focused on "making" his friends do what he wants?

  — What important spiritual implications does learning to accept powerlessness have? What role can recognizing our powerlessness have in our relationship with God initially and throughout life?

Children who grow up hanging on to their omnipotence and never coming to terms with their absolute failure may have difficulty seeing the need for a Savior. Yet the Bible teaches that being powerless is a blessed state: "When we were still powerless, Christ died for the ungodly" (Romans 5:6).

What Is and Isn't the Child's (page 90)

As parent, your job is to help your children sort out what they do and don't have control of and the extent of their power.

- Kids assert their omnipotence in millions of arenas such as chores, clothing styles, privileges and restrictions, and friends.

  — What power struggles have you had with your kids?

  — How did you or do you handle those? How would you like to handle them?

— What lessons about power do you think your children learn from these struggles?

• You probably haven't had willing pupils for these lessons about what your children do and don't have control of and the extent of their power.

— Why don't we human beings like such lessons?

— Why are these lessons important?

Keep a thick skin as you go about your divinely ordained duties of teaching your kids about their limitations.

Power Over Myself (page 90)

A child needs to understand what she can and can't do regarding herself.

• Look again at the table on page 90.

— What do the items listed under "I don't have the power to . . ." remind you about the importance of following through with consequences? About addressing failure in a healthy way?

— What do the items listed under "I do have the power to . . ." remind you about not babying your kids? About the importance of consequences and failure?

- **Denial of Dependency:** Two kinds of dependency often get confused. *Functional dependency* relates to the child's resistance to doing the tasks and jobs in life that are his responsibility. *Relational dependency* is our need for connectedness to God and others.

  — Why is it crucial that you discourage the former and encourage the latter?

  — What are you doing to discourage functional dependency? What consequences are you allowing your child to deal with so that he learns the importance of taking responsibility for himself?

  — What are you doing to encourage relational dependency? Start by noting which of the following are part of your parenting repertoire. Then under "Other" note any different strategies you may have developed.

  Confronting isolation

  Waiting until you are invited to help

  Encouraging him to express his wants, needs, and opinions

  Recognizing and respecting his own rhythm of when he needs to be close and when he needs distance from you

  Not being intrusive and affectionate when he clearly needs to be more separate

Not abandoning him when he needs more intimacy

Encouraging him to share his feedback on family activities

Other:

Children don't like to be reminded that they need anyone but themselves. They want to make their own decisions, solve their own problems, and never have to ask you for help or support. They need to learn from you that mature, healthy people need other people; they don't isolate themselves.

- *Demanding Power over All Choices:* Children think they have the power to do everything they set their mind to. No activity level is too high. They have an omnipotent illusion of their unlimited time and energy. But they can develop boundary problems by overcommitting themselves.

   — When have you seen your child overcommit herself and try to put too many activities into too little time?

— What system have you or could you set up that will break down if she does too much? Consider factoring in such age-appropriate requirements as a B+ average in school, four nights at home with the family each week, an established bedtime, and no signs of fatigue or stress.

Give your child "enough rope to hang herself," so that *she* chooses her destiny, not you. Let her go far enough to experience her lack of omnipotence over her time and energy.

- **Avoiding Consequences:** Part of your little angel's makeup is a criminal mind. He thinks he's powerful enough to avoid the results of his actions. Kids will manipulate, lie, rationalize, and distort to avoid punishment.

  — When have you seen evidence of your child's criminal mind at work? Give an example. How did you respond?

  — What are the consequences for dishonesty in your home? What do you do to reward honesty and encourage your child to admit when he has disobeyed?

Children need to learn to prevent bad consequences by taking control of their actions. When they think they can avoid getting caught, they no longer focus on self-restraint, but on getting away with it. The result is not character maturity, but character pathology. Kids need to learn that living in the darkness of deception is much more painful than living in the light of exposure.

- **Avoiding Failure:** Born perfectionists, kids don't like to be reminded that they are products of the Fall. They often think they have the power to avoid making mistakes or failing. Your children need to learn to grieve their lost perfection, accept their failures, learn from them, and grow.

— Think about how you deal with failure. What kind of model do your kids see in you? What would you like them to see?

— Which of your mistakes or failures are your kids well aware of? Why is it important that they know about such things as your traffic ticket?

Disabuse your child of the notion that she can get around failure. When you talk about her to your friends, include among her achievements the quality of admitting failure.

Power over Others (page 95)

As you help your child give up his delusions of being able to perfectly control himself without failure, you will also need to help him with his similar delusions concerning his power over others.

• Whether due to fear or a desire to be God, children think they have power over their family and friends. Review the chart that shows how you can respond to your children's attempts to have power over others (see page 96).

— Which attempts to have power over others do you see in your kids? Practice saying aloud the appropriate responses.

— Control denies another's freedom; influence respects his freedom. What are you doing, or could you be doing, to teach your children this important difference?

Your child may begin feeling sad that he can't rule his relational world. Grief is good for him, as it allows him to let go of an unrealistic wish. However, help him see that even though he can't have power over others, he isn't helpless, either. Your child needs to learn that he can influence others toward whatever he thinks is important.

- ***The Injured Parent:*** If your child directs his rage or selfishness at you, it can be hurtful. Don't, however, give in to the temptation to use that fact as a way to manipulate the child.

  — Why is it tempting to say something like, "If you yell, you make Mommy sad, and she needs you to help her be happy"? Review the dangers of that approach listed on page 97.

  — When have you let your child know that his words or actions hurt you? How did he respond? What important lesson did that interaction begin to teach?

Children hold onto the idea that they can make others do what they want. They need love, encouragement to take responsibility, and limits on their omnipotence. You are the agent for these three ingredients.

Principles of Power Development (page 98)

Children enter the world with almost no power over themselves. To compensate, they exert enormous energy in controlling their parents. Your job is to gradually increase their power over themselves and decrease their attempts to control you and others. The following principles can help you do that job effectively and with sensitivity.

- ***Stay Connected, No Matter What:*** To help your child tolerate the process of removing her omnipotent power, you will need to stay emotionally present with her. Empathize with her fears of being helpless, her frustration that she can't control her friends' reactions, and her concerns about failure.

  — Why is it important to stay connected to your children no matter what? Why can that connection be difficult to maintain?

— What do you or will you do to show your empathy for your child?

- **Don't Be an Omnipotent Parent:** Help your child accept the limits of her power by accepting the limits of your power. Admit your failure, weakness, and limitations. But also own what power you do have.

    — Which comes more easily: admitting failure or owning your power? What will you do to work on the more challenging task?

    — The statement "I can't make you stop, but I can tell you what will happen if you don't" is a helpful parenting tool. In what current or ongoing situation can you use this tool? What choices and consequences can you structure to help your child choose rightly?

- **Be a Parent Who Makes Free Decisions:** Be "uncontrollable"—that is, a parent whose choices aren't dictated by your child's responses. Her feelings and desires matter to you because you love her. But you are the boss, and you are making the choices you deem best because you are accountable to a higher Boss (2 Corinthians 5:10).

    — What do parents teach a child if they vacillate on a decision when the child freaks out?

    — Why is it wise simply to say no if you're not sure about your child's request?

— If you need your child to behave in a certain way, you have just given her power over you. The key is not to *need* anything such as appreciation, support, respect, or understanding from your child. Where are you getting these needs met—or where could you?

• **Work Toward Giving Your Child Self-Governing Power:** As your child becomes more able to take on responsibility, you should be handing the reins of his life over to him. Your goal is a mutual affection between two adults, not a permanent one-up position.

— How is the statement "I'll always be your parent" both true and false?

— The challenge is to know what you can let your child handle that takes him out of his comfort zone but is not beyond his maturity. Stretch, but don't break him. Where can you be stretching your kids? Be specific for each one.

• **Limit Omnipotence, But Encourage Autonomy:** Children need to know they can't do everything they want. However, this doesn't mean they must be slaves to you or anyone else. They need to develop a sense of autonomy, or free choice over their decisions.

— In what areas of life does (or could) each of your children, whatever their age, enjoy some authentic power? Be specific.

— Consider some decisions (about school, church, finances, or problems) you currently face. On which matters can and will you ask for your child's input? Why is doing that so important? How will you respond to any good ideas he has?

Again, your job as a parent is to gradually increase your child's power over himself and decrease his attempts to control you and others. The principles of power development you just looked at will help your child own what is his and adapt to what is another's.

Conclusion (page 102)

Power can either heal or harm your child.

— What understanding of power is healing?

— What kind of power is harmful in the short-term as well as the long-term?

Your child needs the power that comes from a realistic sense of self-control (healing power), and she needs to give up the desire to have absolute power over herself and her relationships (harmful power). A reality-based understanding of the true power will provide her with a foundation for respecting, setting, and keeping boundaries.

But what does a parent do when children use their power to intrude on the boundaries of others? We will deal with this in the next chapter as we address the Law of Respect.

— Chapter 7 —

I'm Not the Only One Who Matters

The Law of Respect

Respect for others' existence, needs, choices, and feelings does not come naturally. It is learned. Every child comes into the world wanting things and people his way, and he has little regard for what others need. Your task is to cure him of this natural disrespect for the boundaries of other people.

Respecting Others' Boundaries (page 104)

To respect the boundaries of others and to get along with others, children must learn several things:

To not be hurtful to others
To respect the no of others without punishing them
To respect limits in general
To relish others' separateness
To feel sad instead of mad when others' boundaries prevent them from getting what they want

- As we've said before, you can't teach what you don't have. Which, if any, of the five behaviors listed above are you still working on—or could you be working on?

- How will learning these five aspects of respecting others' boundaries make life easier for your kids?

A child does not come into the world doing any of the five behaviors listed above, so your work is cut out for you.

Good Lessons: Don't Hurt Others, Don't Trespass, and Don't Punish Their "No" (page 104)

The best way to teach a child to respect others is for you to have good personal boundaries of your own. This means you are not going to allow yourself to be treated with disregard. If you say no when your children do not respect your personal boundaries or limits, they learn to respect others and their limits. If you don't, they don't.

- Remember eleven-year-old Billy's disrespect of his mom's limits? What did you appreciate about her response?

- *Empathy and Correction:* It is normal for disrespect to occur, but it is not normal for it to continue. The cure is empathy and correction, then consequences.

  — Look again at the four options Billy's mom had. What do you find wise about her responses?

  — Why might these responses be effective?

- *Consequences:* When correction is followed by an apology, sufficient self-correction, and repentance, the child learns respect. If the child does not apologize, repent, and correct himself or if this is a pattern, consequences should follow.

— Again, what do you find wise about the three options for Billy's mom listed here?

— Why is it effective to connect the consequence to the trespass? What is the connection between the trespass and consequence in this example?

— Notice that Billy can't turn anything his mother says into a control issue. Why is that a good move on Mom's part?

— In each response she could choose, Mom is preserving Billy's freedom and his choices, and she is being loving in the process. Identify what choice he is free to make in each case.

• When your child is disrespectful, make sure you stay in control of yourself, as this is what boundaries are all about. But three things need to happen in such a situation.

You will not subject yourself to abuse.
Your child learns that his behavior hurts other people.
If the behavior is not self-correcting, it has to cost the child something.

— What evidence have you seen that your child understands pain? Why is this understanding a key to learning the Golden Rule ("Love your neighbor as yourself"—Matthew 22:39) and establishing boundaries?

— Why is a relational cost logical and helpful when a child has been disrespectful?

Teaching respect involves teaching that "act mean" equals "acting alone" and "act nicely" equals "having someone to listen."

What About Others Besides You? (page 107)

The same principles just outlined apply with people other than you, the parent.

- In general, when possible, don't get involved in children's disputes with one another or with other adults. They need to learn how to work out these disagreements on their own.

    — Explain how letting your child work out her own disagreements shows that you respect her.

    — Remember when Stephen's friends Justin and Robbie went home early? Mary had learned the formula of empathy (compassion) and reality (boundaries and letting Stephen feel the loneliness that resulted from his actions). Why do empathy and reality need to go together rather than letting empathy stand alone?

- The wise parent lets the child's world teach him the lessons of life and then empathizes with his pain. Then he learns to respect the outside world's limits as well as his parents'.

    — Why is letting reality help teach respect for boundaries hard for many parents and perhaps hard for you?

— Sometimes parents do have to help. But why is it important that the child has attempted to work out the problem on his own?

Children must learn that they have to respect other people's property, or it is going to cost them. There can be consequences. But if you work out all of the disputes, children will not learn the problem-solving skills they will need when you are gone.

Respecting Limits in General (page 109)

A limit is generally not loved the first time around—or, for that matter, the first several times around. As the Bible says, "No discipline seems pleasant at the time, but painful" (Hebrews 12:11).

• It's normal for children to protest limits. The problem arises when you get caught up in the protest. You feel as if you have to either defend the limit or punish the protest. Neither option is very helpful. Remember, *the limit is reality if you keep it*.

— Explain why, if you argue with or condemn your protesting child, you become the problem.

— Look again at Scenarios One and Two, the interactions between Kathy and her mother. How did Mom become the problem in Scenario One? Why wasn't that helpful to teaching Kathy lessons for life?

— What does Mom not do in Scenario Two? What life lessons is she teaching here?

— Why is it important that limits are enforced with love?

- If Mom realizes that she owes her child love and empathy only and keeps the limit, then the limit becomes reality. Empathy keeps her out of a power struggle with her child.

  — Empathy is the safe and effective path between the extremes of overidentifying with your child's pain and giving in or getting angry at your child's pain and going to war. Consider times when you may have chosen one or the other of these options. What would a better, more empathic response have been?

  — When protesting limits, your child wants reality to change and wants you to feel the pain he's feeling. Why is it not wise to let the reality change? And why is it important to let him know you are aware of his pain?

When your child protests limits, stay firm and empathic; do not become angry or punitive. Protest will give way to reality, and the child will begin to feel the most important thing he can learn to feel about the limits of reality: sadness.

Sadness and Loss in the Face of Reality (page 112)

Sadness is the sign that protest has given way to reality and that the child has begun to give up the battle. All of us must learn to do this with limits we encounter: Accept the loss of what we want and cannot have and move on.

- The person who learns to move past protest to acceptance has learned an important character lesson: "Life is sad sometimes. You don't always get what you want. Too bad for me. Now I must go on."

  — When have you seen an adult who is stuck protesting a situation in life that he or she cannot change? What has staying stuck cost this person?

— Does your child have an especially tough time accepting your no? Plan a time and a strategy for talking to her about it and offering again the limit and empathy. A sample conversation starter is given on page 113.

Life is sad sometimes, but each of us needs to move on. As parents, we teach our kids this lesson by holding the limits and offering our empathy as we do so.

Respecting Separateness (page 113)

Our freedom and separateness from one another is one of the most important aspects of relationship. We need to be able to respect separateness from the people we love.

- If children have had their needs met and are getting enough connection and love, they need to learn to tolerate separation.

  — What discomfort with separateness do you notice in your children? What is appropriate? How do you respond to it? What signs of discomfort, if any, seem excessive?

  — What discomfort with separateness from your children, if any, do you feel? When does that discomfort arise?

- ***They Need Separateness, Too:*** Allow children their own separateness. To teach them to respect yours, you have to respect theirs. Give them age-appropriate freedom, and do not require them to be at your side at all times. Do not overstep their privacy and space when you don't need to.

  — What are you doing, or could you be doing, to respect the following aspects of your children's lives? Be specific about each child.

  Their Space

Their Time

Their Choice of Friends

Their Money

Their Clothing and Appearance

— What limits are reasonable for each aspect of life? What consequences will you enforce if those limits aren't honored? Again, be specific for each child.

Their Space—Consider safety; common areas in the home; lost items.

Their Time—How will you teach that time limits (mealtimes, the beginning of school, scheduled outings) are real?

Their Choice of Friends—What will you say to your child about friends they are choosing that you would not choose for them? See some suggestions on page 115. If your children's choice of friends is dangerous, you have to act. What will you do?

Their Money—What do parents need to do and *not* do to help their children learn about financial responsibility?

Their Clothing and Appearance—Why are clothes and hairstyles that are not putting your child in danger not worth going to the wall for?

- *Your Separateness from Them:* In addition to your children's separateness from you, you have to be separate from them. Parents who do not have a life apart from their kids teach the kids that the universe revolves around them.

  — What evidence do your children see that you have a life of your own?

  — In what ways do both you and your child benefit from that separateness?

Allowing children their own separateness and respecting it teaches them to respect your separateness. A second lesson comes when you meet your child's needs and then require him to meet his own needs while you meet yours. Empathize with the frustration, but keep the separateness.

How Are You Doing? (page 117)

Children tend to be mirrors in which you can see yourself. They reflect your behavior, habits, attitudes, and ways of seeing and negotiating life.

- In light of that fact, answer the question "What are you doing to respect your children's boundaries and the boundaries of other people?"

- Remember the goals of the Law of Respect? They are listed below along with the questions we asked in the text in order to help you see how well you obey the Law of Respect.

  Don't hurt others—When you hurt your children, do you own the behavior and apologize? Do you tell them you were just thinking of yourself and you're sorry? Do you ask for their forgiveness?

  Respect the no of others without punishing them—When your spouse or children say no to something you want, do you punish them by anger, manipulation, or withdrawal of love? May your children say no to you in matters they should have freedom in? Do you give them choices about managing their own lives? If you want them to play baseball but they like soccer, are they free to say no to you? What if they do not agree with you on all your thoughts about God? Are they free to have separate opinions about their faith?

  Respect limits in general—How do you deal with limits in general? Do you always try to "get around" the rules—and are you modeling that for your children? Do you accept appropriate limits, or are you teaching your children that rules are good for everyone except you?

Relish others' separateness—Do you relish the separateness of others? Are they allowed to have a life apart from you? Are you allowing your children to grow in independence and separateness from you? Do you love their freedom or hate it?

Feel sad instead of mad when you don't always get what you want—When you don't get what you want from your children or others, do you get mad or sad? Do you protest their choices with anger or accept them with sadness? When things do not go your way, do you throw a temper tantrum or do you feel sad and move on?

• What have you seen about yourself in your answers to the questions above? What will you do about those matters in which you see room for growth? Be specific.

The ones who are shown respect are the ones who have the greatest chance of learning respect. You can't ask from your children what you aren't willing to give to them.

The Result (page 119)

The Law of Respect teaches children that the world does not belong to only them and they have to share it with others. They are learning to treat their neighbors as they want to be treated. They don't always get things their way, and they are okay when they don't. They can tolerate not being able to move a limit. They can hear no from others without a fight. And they can tolerate that others have lives separate from them.

• The path toward these results looks like this:

Children protest the limit.
They try to change the limit and punish the one setting it.
You hold to the limit, applying reality and offering empathy.
Children accept the limit and develop a more loving attitude toward it.

— What about walking this path is difficult for you? What keeps you walking the path?

— What limits are the focus of your child's protests these days? What are you saying to show your empathy even as you hold to that limit?

— With what particular limit have you walked the entire path? Put differently, what limit has your child finally accepted? Describe her attitude toward that limit now.

We all know that there are good and bad reasons for showing respect for others. Some people treat others well out of selfishness, guilt, or fear, for example. We want your children to learn loving and responsible behavior out of more positive motivations than these. The next chapter will teach you how to accomplish that.

Chapter 8

Life Beyond "Because I'm the Mommy"

The Law of Motivation

Motives drive our behavior. They are the internal "because" behind the external actions we perform. Motives develop in stages in a child's character. You want your child to do the right things for the right reasons, not simply to avoid punishment.

- Remember the two dads talking about their sons and the trash? The first dad was trying to get his son to mind him and be more responsible. The second dad was on to addressing the motives behind the obedience he was receiving. Is your situation more like the first dad's or the second's? Give specifics for each child to support your answer.

- Once you have your child's attention, motives become crucial.

  — As a rule, what seems to be motivating your child's behavior?

  — Where is your child on the spectrum of obeying to avoid punishment and obeying because it's the right thing to do? To answer that question, let "1" be "behavior dictated by the outside—external restraints and you the parent" and "10" be "owning behavior, doing the right things for the right reasons."

- Consider now how your parenting tactics may be influencing motives.

  — What can be the results, short-term and long-term, when parents resort to guilt messages, threaten a loss of love, or withdraw in silence?

  — What wrong message do such tactics teach a child about her responsibility for her parents' happiness?

Motivations are important in helping your child learn about boundaries. How does a parent help a child develop the right motive for love and good works?

The Goal: Love and Reality (page 122)

The young Swedish girl did her chores without complaining because, in her words, "I like to help; and I also want my sisters to do their jobs!"

- This young girl was talking about motivation. First, she was driven to help by love for her family: She liked to help. Second, she was influenced by the demands of reality: If she did her job, most likely her sisters would, too, and she wouldn't have to do extra work.

  — What are some ways that parents might block the development of this kind of uncomplaining, cooperative child?

  — Which of the ways you just listed interfere with the exchange of love? With the demands of reality?

- "Let each one do just as he has purposed in his heart; not grudgingly or under compulsion; for God loves a cheerful giver" (2 Corinthians 9:7 NASB).

  — What is the difference between (1) being a "cheerful giver" as you do a certain task, and (2) enjoying that task?

  — What burdens do you willingly accept but not necessarily enjoy? What are you modeling for your kids?

  — What burdens, if any at this point, do you see your child accepting fairly willingly but not especially enjoying?

As a parent, you want to develop in the soul of your child a desire to do the right things and to avoid the wrong ones because of empathic concern for others and because of a healthy respect for the demands of God's reality.

The Stages of Motive Development (page 123)

How do you help your children develop good motivation? God has hardwired several stages of influences through which you will need to guide your children.

- Before you start learning more about these four stages, realize that your child needs to be rooted and grounded in love (Ephesians 3:17). Only when you stay connected to her can she grow. Only when she knows that you love her can learning occur.

  — Setting boundaries is a means of loving your child. What will you do to stay connected to her not only in her joys and sorrows but also in her anger and disappointment with you? Be specific. Even jot down some empathic words for times when she is angry or disappointed.

— Detachment is one of the enemies of growth. Consider how detached a parent you are. Do you feel the feelings of love you have for your child? Do you express those feelings? Do you let yourself get close? If you answer no to these questions, where will you go to find supportive relationships in which you can learn to be vulnerable and accessible—and when will you go?

— Conditional love is another enemy of the kind of parent-child contact that enables a child to grow. Are you connecting to your child only when he is good? Are you withdrawing when his behavior is bad? If you have answered yes, what will you do to break this pattern?

Staying connected and assuring her of your love help your child grow. So love first; set limits second.

1. Fear of Consequences: As you begin setting limits and consequences with your child, she will almost certainly test, protest, and express hatred. So stick with your boundaries, be fair but consistent, and empathize with your child's emotional reactions. She will begin to accept the reality that she isn't God, that Mom and Dad are bigger than she is, and that unacceptable behavior is costly and painful to her.

— Remember the talkative six-year-old at the ballgame who responded to the stranger's comment, "Son, you really need to be quiet"? When have you seen your child respond to a similar clear and firm statement?

— What signs, if any at this point, do you see that your child understands the reality that all is not well if he isn't careful?

— What losses and consequences matter to your child?

— One wise father said, "You have to stick to your guns one more time than the child. If he breaks the rule ten thousand times, you have to stay with it only ten thousand and one times, and you'll win." What do you do to maintain the stamina you need to hold the line?

— What do you do to ensure that your child's fear of consequences is not a fear of losing your love?

— Why is it important not to set limits in anger or punitiveness?

— A child needs to understand that his problem is himself, not an enraged parent. Remember Reggie in the grocery store? What caused him to change his behavior?

In this early stage of motivation, the law restrains our out-of-control selves enough so that we can slow down and listen to the message of love. Furthermore, helping your child develop a healthy fear of consequences aligns him with God's reality and makes that reality his friend instead of his nemesis. So when your child tells you that he is only doing his chores because he doesn't want to be grounded, praise him. Then begin helping him with the next step.

2. An Immature Conscience: Drew's "Stop, Drew! Bad, Drew!" was evidence that he was internalizing his experiences with significant relationships and taking them into himself. Internalization is the basis of our ability to love, establish self-control, and have a system of morality and ethics. It shapes our conscience and helps us be aware of right and wrong.

— What evidence, if any at this point, do you see that your child has begun to internalize his experiences with significant people and take them into himself?

— Knowing that we human beings color our experiences with our opinions, wishes, and fears, what do you do to balance the limits you set for your child with expressions of love?

— Being too strict or authoritarian can create a harsh and immature conscience in a child and eventually drive him away from God, from love, from responsibility, and from other people. If you are concerned that you are being too strict, whom will you talk to who knows kids and can offer you some insight?

— At this stage of motive development, avoid the two extremes of either being too strict or pulling away the boundaries. What can happen if a parent pulls away the boundaries? Give two or three possibilities. (The text can help.)

— Remember to be a parent who wants your child's behavior to correspond with the laws of reality, not your own distortions of reality. List some of those laws of reality as well as some of your own distortions of reality that you may be unintentionally passing on to your kids.

As conscience is formed and developed, your child is learning to be motivated to love and be good by internal forces, not just a swat on the behind. He doesn't want to transgress against the internal parent, because it's so much like the real parent. So stay consistent, loving, and attentive to your child's changes. If you have a good-enough attachment to your child and he has accepted your boundaries, your boundaries will become his.

3. *Values and Ethics:* After working with the "voices in his head" for a while, the child begins to take all those experiences and put them into more conceptual form. When he disobeys, he doesn't hear so much "Bad, Drew" as "This is a wrong thing to do." He is beginning to internalize your boundaries more as his own than as an imitation of what you think. This is the beginning of values and ethics.

— At this stage of motive development, your child may begin asking many value-laden questions: "Is this a bad word?" or "Is it okay to watch this TV show?" What such questions, if any, have you been asked by your child?

— Be prepared for these kinds of questions and the opportunities they give you to explain why you believe what you believe about how people should conduct themselves in the world. Why *do* you believe what you believe? Practice explaining the "why" in a way your child can understand.

— Even when a child is wondering about situational versus absolute ethics, the parents aren't done with setting limits and boundaries. When have you seen this in your family or been aware of it in another family? Be specific about how the child needed parenting on both levels.

— Why is it crucial to avoid giving your child guilt and shame messages at this point of motive or conscience development?

At this stage, your child has an operating conscience giving her feedback on her motives for right and wrong. As she continues to work out her own ethics, keep bringing your child back to reality principles like "That goes against what you and we believe."

4. Mature Love, Mature Guilt: As you continue being a source of reality for your child to internalize, he moves and grows beyond the ethical questions of right and wrong to the highest motive: love.

— At the core of his being, your child was created for relationship. What evidence of his concern about relationships have you seen recently? Be specific.

— Explain why empathy is the highest form of love.

— At this stage of motive development, a parent moves from "It's not good to make fun of your overweight classmate" to "How do you think he feels when kids tease him?" In the last week or so, what occasion did you have to talk about relational consequences of your child's actions or words? What did you say? How did he respond?

— Once again, why is it crucial that you avoid overcriticism or withdrawing love? Why do these two options interfere with your child's growth toward being love based and not fear based, being motivated by compassion and not the desire to avoid the pain of criticism or rejection?

Children who are internalizing boundaries need to move beyond "This is right or wrong" to "This hurts others or God." You need to help them freely choose who and how to love and to freely love.

A Final Note (page 133)

In this motivation part of boundary building with your child, don't undervalue any of the three motives for good behavior we have discussed.

- Your child needs to be concerned about the pain of consequences for irresponsibility, the rights and wrongs of his behavior, and what pain his actions may cause his friends and God.

  — What are you doing to teach these three motives for good behavior? List a few of your actions or statements by each.

  The pain of consequences for irresponsibility

  The rights and wrongs of his behavior

  What pain his actions may cause for his friends and God

  — What kind of modeling are you doing? Be specific in each instance.

  The pain of consequences for your own irresponsibility

  Right behavior

  Your consideration of what pain your actions may cause for your friends and God

Even as you model your own awareness of the pain of consequences for your irresponsibility, as you model right behavior, and as you consider and acknowledge what pain your actions may cause your friends and God, create many experiences for your child to internalize them and own them for himself.

All parents must grapple with the reality that boundaries cause pain in our children. That is the subject of the next chapter.

Chapter 9

Pain Can Be a Gift

The Law of Evaluation

Remember the mother of the twelve-year-old girl? Each basic limit or consequence I (Dr. Cloud) suggested would not work for one reason or another.

- What excuses, if any, for not enforcing limits are you using or have you used in the past?

- What often keeps people from enforcing limits and consequences for their children? What, if anything, is keeping you?

This mom did not know how to evaluate her daughter's pain. In short, she did not know the difference between *hurt* and *harm*. The boundaries I was suggesting would definitely hurt her daughter, but they would not harm her.

- When has helping your child not felt very good to you? Be specific.

- When has helping your child hurt her? More specifically, when did she feel sadness or wounded pride or experience the loss of something she values? Why did you (if you did) hold fast to the limit?

Harm means actual injury by wounding her person or, through judgment or attack or abandonment, not providing something she needs. The effective parent must learn the distinction between hurt and harm if a child is ever going to develop boundaries.

Pain and Growth (page 136)

Lesson number one in parenting and life is "Growth involves pain." Lesson number two is "Not all pain produces growth." Learning to tell the difference is the key to having someone stay on the bottom or grow past where he or she is.

- "No pain, no gain" was the basketball team's mantra as players conditioned, trained, and practiced, sometimes past the point they thought they could endure.

  — If you are independent, you are used to doing things that "hurt" so you can receive something you desire. Give a recent example from your life.

  — When I had mononucleosis and missed a month of school, I was overwhelmed with the amount of work I had to catch up on. But my mom knew it would not harm me to keep going. How did your parents respond to hurts you wanted to avoid? Give one example from your childhood. Be sure to mention what you gained from walking through the hurt or what lesson (helpful or otherwise) you learned from being given an escape.

- When I was four years old, a childhood bone disease caused me to lose the use of my left leg for two years. At times I had to use a wheelchair, and at other times I wore restrictive braces and walked on crutches.

  — What do you appreciate about the way my mom handled those tough years?

  — I tried to manipulate my mom and dad into not allowing me to suffer the pain of learning self-sufficiency. But they kept their limits, and we made it through. In what specific area of life is your child facing the pain of learning self-sufficiency? What can you learn from my experience about your role as a parent?

The parent who hears his child's every cry or complaint as the ultimate concern will never develop boundaries and character in that child. When your children cry about homework, chores, or a missed opportunity because they did not do their part, what are you going to do? How you answer this question will have a tremendous effect on the course of your child's life.

Four Rules for Evaluating Pain (page 138)

When your children cry or complain, keep in mind the following rules for evaluating their pain.

* ***Rule #1: Don't Let Your Child's Pain Control Your Actions:*** If your child is controlling your decisions by protesting your boundaries, you are no longer parenting with purpose. Furthermore, clue number one that a child will not develop self-control is when the *parent* does not have self-control in enforcing the rules.

   — How was Terri letting Josh's protests define right from wrong?

   — What are some of the lessons we teach our kids when we give in to their crying?

   — The child's protest does not define either reality or right from wrong. In what current parenting situation will this truth help you stand strong and empathize with your child's pain but enforce the limit?

Frustration and painful moments of discipline help a child learn to delay gratification, one of the most important character traits a person can have. If you rescue your children from their anger at your boundary, you can plan on more anger at later limits.

- **Rule #2: *Keep Your Pain Separate from Your Child's:*** As Terri and I ultimately discovered, she was trying to make her own pain go away. Having known much pain as a child, she was now *overidentifying* with her son's pain.

  — Could you be overidentifying with your child's pain? Consider your childhood and your reactions to your child's sadness. What specific situation suggests you may be overidentifying?

  — If you are overidentifying, whom will you turn to for support as you learn to keep your experience separate from your child's? Who can remind you of the truth that your child's pain is not as intense as the pain you knew growing up?

Keep your own sadness about your children's pain separate from theirs. "Each heart knows its own bitterness, and no one else can share its joy" (Proverbs 14:10). We all must endure our own pain.

- **Rule #3: *Help Your Child See That Life Is Not About Avoiding Pain, But About Making Good Pain an Ally:*** Basically, we change when the pain of staying the same becomes greater than the pain of changing. Therefore life is not about avoiding suffering. Life is about learning to suffer well.

  — Look again at the chart that shows what problems a pain avoider faces (page 142). What do you see about yourself in that chart? Identify areas where you can grow.

  — What did your parents teach you about frustration and adversity? What have been the consequences or benefits of those lessons?

— In teaching your children that pain can be good, which of the following have you been able to model recently or could you start modeling today? Be brief about the circumstances. Focus on what your kids may have seen in how you handled the situation.

Facing problems

Being sad but continuing onward

Empathizing with them about how hard it is to do the right thing and then still requiring it

Problems come from the tendency to avoid the pain of the momentary struggle, the pain of self-discipline and delaying gratification. If we learn to lose what we want in the moment, to feel sad about not getting our way, and then to adapt to the reality demands of difficult situations, joy and success will follow. We need to hear what a friend of mine tells her son: "I know, Tim. Livin's hard—but I believe you can do it."

- ***Rule #4: Make Sure the Pain Is the Pain of Maturing, Not the Pain of Need or Injury:*** Children's behavior often sends a message, and parents need to evaluate the pain to find out whether it is the pain of frustration or the pain of need or injury. The four-year-old daughter of my friend was dawdling not to defy her dad but because she was missing her mom.

  — Review the valid reasons why older children sometimes misbehave (page 144). Which of these, if any, may explain some misbehavior in your home?

— Consider whether you may be the source of your child's pain by reviewing the list of things parents do to exasperate or embitter their kids (Ephesians 6:4; Colossians 3:21).

Exercising too much control over your children's lives so that they have no power over or choice in their lives

Disciplining with anger and guilt instead of empathy and consequences

Not meeting their needs for love, attention, and time

Not affirming their successes, but only commenting on their failures

Being too perfectionistic about their performance instead of being pleased with their effort and with the general direction in which they are going

What, if anything, have you done to exasperate your children or embitter them? If that hasn't happened, consider how your children may perceive or experience your regular interactions. Are you at risk of exasperating or embittering them? If exasperation (either past or potential) is the case, what will you do today to improve the relationship?

When you evaluate your child's pain, make sure, first, that it is not caused by a real injury or trauma or something other than the real need for discipline and, second, that you have not caused it. Normal parents will cause pain from time to time, but they will see their fault and apologize.

Consider It All Joy (page 145)

James 1:2-4 reads, "Consider it pure joy, my brothers, whenever you face trials of many kinds, because you know that the testing of your faith develops perseverance. Perseverance must finish its work so that you may be mature and complete, not lacking anything."

- God does not rescue us from our struggles and the pain of learning discipline and perseverance. In fact, God disciplines those he loves, just as a father disciplines his children (Hebrews 12:5-10).

    — What lessons have you learned from the struggles of your life?

    — What kind of pain have you experienced as you have learned discipline and perseverance?

    — Are you willing to let your child experience the pain that teaches discipline and perseverance? Why or why not?

- Struggle refines the character of the child. Waiting for the reward makes a child learn how to perform. Trials and pain teach us the lessons that build the character we will need to negotiate life.

    — What signs do you see, if any at this point, that struggle has taken off or started to wear down some of your child's rough edges? Be specific about the struggle as well as its refining work in your child's character.

Evaluate your children's pain. If they are in need or injured, run to their rescue. But if they are protesting reality's demands for maturing to the next level, empathize with that struggle, manage it well, but let them go through it to the end. Later, they will thank you.

When children learn to value the pain of life instead of avoid it, they are ready to solve their problems. But what you want is for the child to be proactive in the process. In the next chapter we show how that happens.

Chapter 10

Tantrums Needn't Be Forever

The Law of Proactivity

When Derek struck out and on another occasion when he missed a catch, I (Dr. Townsend) realized that he was avoiding any problems he encountered in the play. He had never had to deal with frustration, failure, or skill building. Learning was pre-empted by his reactive tantrum. Also, I saw that although Derek had the problem, his friends were paying for his immaturity.

- The next time I saw Derek, I talked to him about his pattern and told him the new rule: "It's okay to be upset in a game, and we'll help you learn what is hard for you, but it's not okay to leave. If you do, you can't come back for the rest of the game."

— What was logical and appropriate about this consequence?

— Where do you see empathy in the wording?

— After two occasions when I had to impose the limit, Derek was in a game and was tagged out at second base. He protested, but this time he quieted down and kept playing. What surprised or encouraged you about Derek's reaction?

Derek illustrates a problem in child rearing and boundaries that exists, at some level, in all of us: the struggle between reactivity and proactivity, between lashing out in protest or responding maturely to problems. Your job is to help children develop the ability to set appropriate boundaries, yet without exploding or being impulsive.

When Kids React (page 149)

Children don't come by deliberate, thought-out action naturally.

- They don't accept no easily, and they give up quickly. They react to stress rather than act upon it. Although the child may well be protesting something wrong or bad, his reactions are still immature.

  — Which of the following reactive behaviors have you seen your child adopting?

    Tantrums

    Oppositionalism

    Whining

    Impulsivity

    Fighting and violence

  — Consider this three-part description of reactivity in children:

    Children's responses are reactions, not actions: their behavior is determined by some external influence, not by their values or thoughts.

    Children's reactions are oppositional: they take a stance against what they don't like, but not for what they desire or for values.

    Children's reactive boundaries are not value driven.

- What do these facts suggest about your job description as a parent? Specifically, what do these facts say to you about the importance of teaching your child self-control?

Children act spontaneously and unwisely. If parents don't help them learn self-control, children become like the hotheaded man in the Bible: "A quick-tempered man does foolish things" (Proverbs 14:17).

Reactive Boundaries: Necessary But Insufficient (page 151)

At this point you may think that reactive boundaries are bad for your child. The reality is, however, that they have their place in his development. Let's take a look at what they are about.

- *Necessary:* Children's reactive boundaries are necessary for their survival and growth. Children need to be able to protest what they are against, do not like, or fear. Being able to protest helps the child define herself, keep the good in and the bad out, and develop the ability to take responsibility for her own treasures.

  — When has your child's protest been appropriate to a dangerous situation or to having a need met?

  — When has your child's protest of a problem or obstacle not been appropriate— that is, the problem was neither dangerous nor evil?

  — Protest identifies the problem, but it doesn't solve the problem. Reactive boundaries signal that something needs to be dealt with, but proactive boundaries fix something that is broken. Reactive boundaries lead to mature, loving boundaries through a sequence of abilities and skills.

— Review those stages (page 153) and identify where your children are on this path.

— What support and structure are you as parents offering your children for their individual journeys along this path? Consider what you have been learning in this study of boundaries.

- ***Insufficient:*** Reactive boundaries protect and help separate your child from bad things, but they are insufficient for a successful adult life.

  — Children who never move beyond reactive boundaries develop a victim identity. They look at most of their struggles in life as coming from the outside, not from inside themselves. Thus, they are forever prohibited from improving their lives because no problem that originates outside of us is really solvable. What can parents do to keep their kids from acquiring this damaging perspective on the source of our problems?

  — Reactive boundaries are insufficient because children need to grow up to be defined by more than what they hate. What problems might result if a child never gets beyond this point?

  — What are you doing, or could you be doing, to encourage your child to think for himself, disagree, and talk about his feelings while accepting your authority? Be specific.

Reactivity helps your child seek and find his boundaries. But once he has found them, once he knows what he doesn't like, he isn't free to indulge his feelings by seeking revenge, avoiding dealing with those feelings, or getting out of his responsibilities.

Proactive Boundaries (page 154)

On the first day of youth soccer, I can tell which kids have reactive boundaries and which have proactive ones. Those with reactive boundaries don't like instruction, get into poking fights with each other, irritate quickly, and get tired of drills they don't do well at immediately. Those with proactive boundaries pay attention, make mistakes and learn from them, and speak up if they don't like something or if they need something. Here's more about what proactive boundaries look like.

- *Proactive boundaries go beyond problem identification to problem solving*—Your child needs to know that in protesting, she has only identified the problem, not solved it. She needs to use these feelings to motivate her to action, to address the issue at hand.

  — Consider a common cause of your child's tantrums. What can you say to empathize and still enforce the limits? What more appropriate expression of her feelings could you suggest if she doesn't come up with any ideas on her own?

  — Why is empathy a better path than insisting that a child conform both in behavior and attitude?

- *Proactive boundaries encompass both what the child is for and against*—While reactive boundaries help children identify what is "not me" and what they don't like, they also need to know what they love.

  — What does your child feel safe protesting? What teaching would you like to introduce the next time he expresses his dislikes?

— What did you learn from the way Mom and Dad handled Taylor and his responses to them?

— When have you noticed your child acting out of a sense of gratitude, warmth toward his family, or a concern for the feelings of others—indications that proactive boundaries are in effect?

• *Proactive boundaries mean others can't control the child*—Children who have reactive boundaries and live in protest are still dependent on other people. Children with proactive boundaries, however, view life, make decisions, and respond to the environment according to their own internal values and realities.

— In what situation, if any, can you help your reactive child see that as long as he is giving up time and energy reacting, the person to whom he is reacting is in control of his precious time?

— Think again about Brittany and Jan. What did this real-life example show you about how to help a sensitive child develop proactive boundaries?

— The old saying goes "If you want to fix the child, fix the parent." In what ways, if any, might you—like Jan—be inviting your child to be dependent on you rather than learning to take responsibility for her own emotions?

- *Proactive boundaries are not about revenge and fairness, but about responsibility*—
Reactive boundaries operate under the law "an eye for an eye." Proactive boundaries are more concerned with higher motives, such as responsibility, righteousness,
and love for others. Put differently, with reactive boundaries you fight the friend
who constantly bugs you. With proactive boundaries, you decide you don't need
that kind of friend.

  — When, if ever, have you seen your child not let himself be taken advantage of, a
  sign of proactive boundaries? Why is the next step—being a crusader against
  every bully on the playground—not an indication of proactive boundaries?

  — When has the issue of fairness arisen in your home? What is helpful about the
  response, "You're right—lots of things aren't fair"?

Proactive boundaries encourage the child to solve problems, not just complain
about them; define what he loves, not just what he hates; get out from under the control of others; and focus on getting his needs met, not judging the world for not being
fair to him.

The Skills of Proactive Boundaries (page 161)

Proactive boundaries are learned over time, developed as fine gold from the ore of
reactive boundaries. You need to teach your child several skills that, when joined with
her protest stance, will enable her to be a self-controlled, value-based person. Timing is
important. Don't go over the skills listed here until your child is in a teachable place,
generally after several failed assaults on your boundaries.

- What boundary issues can you anticipate having to deal with in the next week or so?
Prepare to address one or more of the following skills in a teachable moment.
Review the descriptions given in the text (pages 161–62) and then thoughtfully plan
how you will teach the skill.

Pausing instead of reacting

Observation of himself

Perspective on her feelings as well as other people's feelings

Problem solving

Reality that calls for negotiation and compromise

Initiative to be proactive to solve or avoid the problem

• Don't be a Lone Ranger Mom or Dad. Whom can or do you go to for solid parent-ing advice?

As a parent you need to worry if your child has never had a tantrum of if he has had too many. If your child falls into the second category and seems stuck in a reactive stage, you can help him mature his reactive boundaries into love-and-reality-based proactive boundaries, helping him take control of his life, character, and morality.

If anything destroys honesty and self-control in your child, it is gossip or what psy-chologists call triangulation. And gossip tends to spring from envy, an issue we will look at next.

Chapter 11

I Am Happier When I Am Thankful
The Law of Envy

If you have a child, you have dealt with envy. Envy is the basest human emotion, and to some degree, all humans envy. The saddest aspect of the matter is the emptiness envious people continually feel. Nothing is good enough; nothing fulfills them. Contentment is forever missing from their lives.

• Children learn what they live with. Review the "Envious people . . ." list (page 163). What, if anything, do you see about yourself in this description? If you recognize envy as something you need to resolve, what will you do toward that end?

Envy is the perpetual "wanting more." Normal to some degree, this problem should be disappearing as a child grows in accepting boundaries. The purpose of this chapter is to teach you how to transform normal childhood envy into acceptance, gratitude, and contentment.

Entitlement Versus Gratitude (page 164)

Entitlement is when someone feels as if people owe him things or special treatment simply because he exists. People with this character trait feel entitled to privileges, special treatment, things other people have, respect, love, or whatever else they want. And when they do not get what they want, they feel that the one who is not giving it to them is "wrong."

• Children first feel entitled to be in control. Then they feel they are entitled not to suffer, to work, or to adapt to rules and boundaries. Later, they feel entitled to what

113

others have. What evidence of this developmental sense of entitlement have you seen in your kids?

- The opposite of envy and entitlement is gratitude. Gratitude comes from the feeling of freely receiving things, not because we deserve them, but because someone has graced us with them. We feel a thankfulness grounded in love, and we cherish what we have received.

  — Who among your friends is a truly grateful person? What contributes or gives rise to that gratitude? What is it like to spend time with this person?

  — What has taught or is teaching you to be grateful?

The two states—envy and gratitude—have little to do with what a person actually receives. They have more to do with the character of the person. Parents need to help children work through their feelings of entitlement and envy and move to a position of gratitude.

The Problem of Two Mommies and Two Daddies (page 165)

In a child's mind, there are two mommies, not one, and two daddies, not one. There is the good mommy or daddy who gratifies them and relieves their stress and the bad one who frustrates their wishes.

- Consider what goes on inside children. When children are getting what they want, they see themselves as *entitled* to what they are receiving; when they are being frustrated, they see themselves as *victims* of the "bad mom." As children experience both having their needs met and being frustrated with limits, they slowly merge the two images of themselves and others.

— Look back over yesterday. When did your child have her needs met? How did she respond to being cared for? Put differently, what evidence did you see of gratitude developing?

— When did your child encounter limits yesterday and know the frustration of not getting what she wanted? How did she respond to not getting what she wanted? What evidence did you see of a sense of entitlement or being a victim?

• As this combination of gratification and frustration occurs a few million times, children gain a secure sense of the world's being "not perfect" in gratifying them all the time, but "good enough" in giving them what they need. Children endure enough frustration to become grateful for what they receive as they find out they are not entitled to everything they want.

— Consider your path from entitlement to gratitude. What events contributed to your growth toward gratitude? Was there an "aha!" moment of realizing that you are not entitled to things simply because you exist? If so, describe that moment.

— What does your family life in general teach your child, through both spoken words and modeling, about gratitude?

The balance of gratification and frustration tempers the extremes of neediness and entitlement. In addition, a child learns to not see himself as a victim when he's deprived, nor does he see others as bad when they do not do what he wants. He develops a balanced view of himself and others.

Giving, Limiting, and Containing (page 167)

To give your children a balanced sense of themselves and others, you must gratify needs and some wants, and frustrate others. The three skills necessary to do this are giving, limiting, and containing.

- *Giving:* Giving is the gratification of needs and wants. The most important gratification is the one for love, connection, and care. Each age offers parents opportunities to give toward particular needs.

  — At which stage is each of your children?

  An infant with basic needs for food, care, warmth, and safety?

  A little older child, whose fears need to be gratified with reassurance?

  Older yet, who needs freedom, space, and some control and choices and who is learning what he wants and how to ask for it?

  Still older, who wants to have things, activities, and resources (money and opportunities) to explore their skills and talents?

  — What are you doing, or could you be doing, to meet your child's specific needs? Where are you giving "bountifully" to your children so that they can be healthily "weaned" for life?

Children need to learn that the world is a place where they can receive things and fulfill their talents and dreams. At the same time, they are learning that they must be responsible and wise. Give to them, meet their needs for love and affection, and give them opportunities to grow and the equipment they need to carry out their life tasks.

- **Limiting:** Limiting is making sure children do not get too much or do not get inappropriate things. It is making sure that their wish to be in control of everything is not gratified. In addition, limiting is disciplining and managing their choices and consequences. It has to do with the way you live out the word no and make it reality.

  — Again, consider the age of your children and evaluate how well you're doing with setting and enforcing limits.

    Infancy: She is limited by physical existence, yet learning that she has had all she needs and now just has to go to sleep.

    Toddlerhood: *No* has meaning; they are learning that they are not entitled to everything they want, that they are not in control, and that they need to use words and not whine or manipulate to get what they need.

    Later childhood: When they want toys they can't have, they learn the world isn't going to just give them what they want. They learn they have to earn what they want. They learn that they won't get something simply because a friend or sibling has it; they learn that life is not fair if they define fairness as equality.

    Teenage years: You need to enforce limits on how you will allow them to treat you as they take on the guardian and manager role for themselves.

  — Throughout the developmental spectrum, limiting your children is important in overcoming envy and entitlement. Read again the statements about limits on page 171 of the text. Which statements about the importance of limits are especially significant to you? In light of what these statements say, why are limits a crucial way by which you love your child and meet her greatest needs?

You must not reinforce your children's feeling that they are entitled to have whatever they want, to do whatever they want, or to treat people however they wish. If you have good limits along with balanced gratification, they will find out they do not own the world. So do not rob your children of limits. Otherwise, they will have the lifelong burden of thinking they are God. That is a role at which they are sure to fail.

- *Containing:* Containing is helping a child to work through her feelings about a limit and to internalize that limit as character. Containing, then, is the addition of love, understanding, and structure to limits.

  — Anger is a typical reaction when a child encounters a limit. What dangerous message is communicated if the limit is removed because of that protest?

  — The staying power of the limit breaks the grandiosity of the child. What role does empathy play at this moment?

  — Look again at (and perhaps even memorize) the five empathic statements listed on page 172. What important message do statements like these communicate to a child who has bumped into an immovable limit?

Remember, as your children learn limits, they are losing more than just what they wanted. They are losing their entire view of life; they are learning that they are not in control. Expect them to hate this for a little while.

Courage to Be Hated (page 173)

The parent who cannot tolerate being hated will not be able to provide the reality the child needs to overcome feeling entitled. Love and limits are the most important qualities for a parent. The ability to tolerate being hated and seen as "bad" is a parent's next most important quality.

- Think back to times when you hated your parents. Now that you're on the other side, what do those scenes teach or remind you about the dynamic of a child hating his parents?

- How well do you tolerate being hated? What will you do to take care of yourself in preparation for your child's hatred? After that hatred has been expressed?

As God did for Job, you need to be able to contain the protest, stay connected, not strike back, and remain the parent.

When "Thank You" Does Not Come (page 173)

Expressing gratitude is a very important aspect of development. If it is not appearing, it needs to be addressed.

- A child who is not expressing thanks needs to be talked to and limited. He is taking things for granted. Let him know that this is not appreciated by others.

  — Are you seeing your children develop a grateful attitude? Support your answer with specific examples of their words and actions.

  — As you work on helping your child express gratitude, share your feelings even as you enforce your limits with statements like the five listed on page 174. What do you appreciate about those statements? Which ones do you anticipate being able to use?

- If you feel like a martyr or feel that, in light of your sufferings, you deserve pity, you may be making your child feel guilty, and that will interfere with teaching genuine gratitude. How will you deal with your feelings first so that you can talk to your child about gratitude without adding guilt?

Help your child learn to express gratitude by setting forth your own limits in not allowing yourself to be taken for granted.

Distinguishing Between Envy and Desire (page 174)

One of the neat things about being a parent is helping your child achieve a desire. How wonderful to help a child reach a goal or attain something he wants!

- Think about the two stories of teenagers and their cars.

  — When, if ever, have you worked hard and waited long to reach a goal? What motivated you? What was your attitude toward the goal once you achieved it?

  — When, if ever, have you been given something without earning it and for the wrong reasons? What were the motives or concerns of the giver(s)? What was your attitude (long-term as well as short-term) toward the gift?

- Parents would do well to determine which of their child's wishes come from envy and which are heartfelt desires.

  — What heartfelt desires—those which have stood the test of time—have your children shared with you? What did you do to support your children?

— How have you handled, or how would you like to handle, your children's desires that arise from envy?

Let the envious wishes die and help your child achieve the ones that come from the heart.

It's Your Yard (page 175)

Desire moves our children (and us) to work. Envy just burns within.

- Seeing things we want but don't have and recognizing who we want to be but aren't yet can motivate us to work toward those goals.

  — When have you looked at the world, seen things you want, and gone to work to get those things? When have your children seen you do this?

  — When have you looked at your abilities, possessions, or skills, been sad about what's missing, and gotten to work to fill those holes? When have your children seen you do this?

- If you have good limits and boundaries, you will empathize with your child's longing, help him to plan to reach the goal, and encourage him. If you don't give in to his envy, you have taught him one of the most important lessons in life: His lack is his problem.

  — When have you seen your child look at the world outside himself, see things he wants, and be motivated by this desire to work? Or when have you noticed your child look at his abilities, his possessions, or his skills, feel sad at what's missing, and be moved to work?

— In that situation, what supporting role did you play for your child or, currently, what supporting role could you play?

When a child realizes that his wants and desires are his problem, he can ask for help, pray, learn, work, or do whatever he needs to do. But his lack and the solution are his problem before God. No one should solve things for him.

The Paradox (page 176)

Envy is a huge paradox in life. Envious people think they deserve everything, but in the end have nothing. They are not able to own, cherish, or be thankful for the things they possess. What they do not possess, possesses them.

• Explain how envy is basically pride.

• The envious want more, and get less. The grateful are thankful for what they already have, and receive more. When have you seen this paradox revealed in real life?

Help your child to become a humble, grateful person. But remember, swallowing the pride sandwich is a big bite and can only be done with a lot of love to wash it down. Then he can get busy being active to solve his problems, which is the subject of the next chapter.

Chapter 12

Jump-starting My Engine

The Law of Activity

Working at a children's home in Texas after I (Dr. Townsend) graduated from college, I noticed differences between us houseparents. Basically, there were two extremes: the "best friend" type and the "control freak" type. The best houseparents were somewhere in the middle: They were both relational and structured.

- The rule of thumb for success was this: *When respect came before friendship, activity resulted. When friendship came before respect, passivity resulted.*

    — When, if ever, have you observed this truth in real life?

    — Why do you think passivity results when friendship comes before respect?

    — At this point of the chapter, what does this pair of sentences suggest to you about your parenting?

We human beings are self-centered and passive about taking responsibility. We need the law (limits and consequences) to get our attention. Then, when we realize that we aren't God and that passivity will bring us pain, we get busy working on life, and God gives us grace to help and support us.

The Gift of Activity (page 178)

One of the greatest gifts you can give your child is to help build in her a tendency toward activity. To be active is to take initiative, to make the first move. A child needs to understand that the solution to her problems and the answer to her needs always begins not with someone else, but with her.

- *Do not confuse dependency with passivity.* We are designed to be actively dependent on God and others all our lives. *By the same token, do not confuse activity with self-sufficiency.* Active people don't attempt to do everything on their own.

  — Take a look at yourself in light of these italicized truths. What do you see about yourself? Where do you fall on the passivity/activity spectrum? Do you let yourself be healthily dependent? Do you try to be unhealthily self-sufficient? What might your model be teaching your kids?

  — Activity means doing all you can do, then aggressively seeking what isn't in you to complete you. In what area of your life has this been or could this be your approach? Be specific.

  — Your child needs to actively let his needs be known, protest the bad, hold up his end of his friendships, do his chores and schoolwork, and gradually shoulder more and more of the load of his life as he matures. Take time to evaluate what you are modeling in each of these areas:

  Letting needs be known

  Protesting the bad

Holding up your end of your friendships

Doing your chores

- Children who are active have an ideal chance of learning to respond to boundaries correctly. Like an untamed bronco, they use their wills to buck against your limits and consequences until they learn to pay attention to realities other than their own.

  — Review the list of benefits your child receives from God's gift of activity (page 179). Which of these statements about the importance of activity do you find especially significant or challenging? Why?

  — Look, too, at the Bible's confirmation of this Law of Activity (page 179). What other verses, if any, would you add to support the assertion that, being made in God's image, we are to be active, problem-solving initiative-takers as he is?

As a parent your job is to set the limits and enforce the consequences in love. Your child's job is to test the limits many times with her active aggression and thereby learn about reality, relationships, and responsibility. It's the divinely ordered system.

The Problem of Passivity (page 180)

Passivity, or being inert or nonresponsive, is the opposite of activity and initiative. Passivity in children is a major obstacle to boundary development. Passive kids are in a holding pattern, waiting on someone or something. When children are passive, they are no longer learning to be stewards of themselves.

- Passive kids are unable to make use of the trying-failing-learning process that teaches them boundaries.

  — When have you seen your child step up to the plate—or choose not to?

  — Does your child have difficulty making friends and finding interests and passions? Is she easily influenced or controlled by more aggressive friends? Does she tend to "go along to get along"? "Yes" answers suggest a tendency toward passivity.

- Evil grows in the absence of active limits. The passive person is an unwitting ally of evil by not resisting it. When have you seen evil grow in the absence of active limits?

- Don't confuse passivity with patience, which is a positive trait, namely, restraining our impulse to do God's job for him (James 5:8). Consider your answers to the questions at the beginning of this section and any tendency toward passivity you may have noticed in your child. What evidence of passivity, if any, do you see in your child? Could you be confusing passivity with patience? Whom will you ask for another opinion?

The message of the Bible concerning activity and passivity is, as the Marines say, "A bad decision is better than no decision." Active kids learn and mature more quickly than passive ones, giving the parent more raw material to work with.

What Can You Do About a Passive Child? (page 181)

If you are the parent of a passive child, you have a double problem. Passive kids have the same boundary problems of irresponsibility or resistance to ownership that active kids do, but it's harder to engage them in the learning process.

- Children exhibit passivity in a variety of ways, among them:

  Procrastination
  Ignoring
  Lack of initiative and risk-taking
  Living in a fantasy world
  Passive defiance
  Isolation

Review the definitions of these behaviors (pages 181–82) and note any that you see consistently in your child.

Children have struggles in this area for several reasons. The following are some of the root causes. Note the ways you can help your passive children develop the activity needed to gain their own boundaries.

- *Fear:* Your children may be nonresponsive because of underlying fears or anxieties that paralyze them from taking initiative. Overwhelming fear causes children to take a protective and defensive stance toward the challenges of life.

  — *Closeness*—Some children are afraid of being close and vulnerable with others. What are you doing, or could you be doing, to make school, church, sports, arts, and other social activities a normal and expected part of family life? What do you do to support your child before and after she enters a social situation?

  — *Conflict*—Some kids are actively involved when everything is going okay, but become afraid and passive around anger or conflict. What are you doing, or could you be doing, to normalize conflict and pain, to teach your child that conflict is okay and that she will survive it? What are you modeling in this regard?

— *Failure*—Afraid of making a mistake, many kids these days prevent themselves from taking initiative and thereby reduce the chance that they will fail. What are you doing, or could you be doing, to normalize failure for your children? What stories of your failures are they aware of? When, if ever, have they seen you fail and laugh at yourself?

• *Inability to Structure Goals:* Some kids sink into passive stances because they have problems thinking through what steps to take to get what they want. Their tolerance for frustration is also generally low.

— What evidence have you seen that your child can think through steps for getting from point A to point B?

— What chores that have some complexity (cooking, cleaning, grocery shopping, yard maintenance, even home repairs) can you give your child to help him develop confidence in his ability to perform?

• *Clairvoyant Expectations:* A child may feel he shouldn't have to ask for what he needs, on the assumption that you should know before he asks. As children grow up, they need to let their needs to be clearly known.

— How easily does your child communicate his needs? When, for instance, has he gotten upset because you didn't ask the right questions, you forgot something he wanted, or you didn't understand why he was unhappy?

— What does your child see in his parents about how to make needs known?

— When will you explain, "Even though I love you very much, I can't read your mind. If you don't use your words and say what you want, you will not get a response"? What else might you do to let your child know you really want to help him meet his needs and solve his problems?

• *Conflicted Aggression:* Some kids are not innately passive. They are aggressive in some areas and nonresponsive in others. These kids have the necessary active, assertive ingredients, but they have difficulty accessing them in certain areas.

— In what areas of life (some functional, some relational) is your child active? In what areas is he passive?

— The rule of thumb here is "You don't get the goodies until you make real efforts in your problem areas." Guided by this rule, what will you do to help your child get beyond his passivity in certain areas? Be specific.

• *Laziness:* Sometimes kids are passive because they have little "anticipatory anxiety." The future holds no fear for them. They know someone else will take care of any problems that arise. They lack fear of consequences.

— At the root of most lazy kids lies an enabling parent. Kids will be as passive as you train them to be. What degree of passivity is your training allowing? To answer that question, ask yourself whether running the household is a team effort or a token effort on your children's part? Is their income tied to performance at home and school?

— What would another parent say about your expectations of your child? Ask! Find out whether another parent thinks you're doing too much and your child too little.

— Set limits and consequences for laziness today. Outline them here and set a time for explaining them to your child.

• *Entitlement:* A major cause of passivity in children is an entitled attitude, a demand for special treatment. Such children feel they deserve to be served by virtue of their existence. All kids have a certain amount of entitlement (see chapter 11), but some have too much, as we see in the account of sixteen-year-old Sean.

— God's solution for entitlement is humility (Philippians 2:3). To help your child, what will you do to frustrate his grandiose feelings while satisfying his real needs?

— To counter your child's sense of entitlement, don't go overboard praising required behavior. But do go overboard when your child confesses the truth, repents honestly, takes chances, and loves openly. In light of this guideline, what events from the past week would you handle differently in the future? Also, what changes in your standard responses to your child, if any, would you do well to make in light of this guideline?

• *Clinical Issues:* Sometimes childhood passivity can be a symptom of an underlying emotional disorder or of drug and alcohol problems. If you suspect these issues, what will you do to find a therapist experienced with kids your child's age so you can get a clinical opinion?

Principles of Developing an Active Child (page 188)

Whether or not your child is naturally passive, you will need to take a role in helping her become a seeker and grower. You are the primary solution in enforcing the Law of Activity. Here is what you do:

- *Become an Active Person, Not Just a Parent:* A child needs to internalize a model of someone who has a life of her own.

  — What are you doing, or could you be doing, to let your child know you have interests and relationships that don't involve her? What trips do you take and what activities do you pursue without her?

  — What are you doing to show your child that you take active responsibility in meeting your own needs and solving your own problems?

- *Work Through Any Enabling of Your Child's Passivity:* Don't confuse your love with rescuing your child from himself.

  — Whom will you ask this week about whether you are stretching your child's growth muscles sufficiently?

  — Are you avoiding setting limits in the academic, work, social, spiritual, and behavioral areas of your child's life? Are you afraid of discussing these problems because of possible conflict? Is your home a retreat from responsibility, or a place of movement and growth? What do your answers suggest about what changes you need to make? Be specific.

- ***Require Initiative and Problem Solving:*** Your child's tendency is to let you do all the work. It is your fault if you do it.

  — What situations can you expect to encounter this week in which you could say something like "I'm sorry, but that's your responsibility. I hope you solve your problem; it sounds difficult, but I'm pulling for you"?

  — What kind of response to "It's your responsibility . . ." do you expect? What will you do to show empathy yet hold the limit?

- ***Teach Your Child to Move Toward Relationship:*** Passive children often avoid relationships, which are one of the good resources God designed to help them live life.

  — What can you do or say to help your child see that relationship is the source of many things—comfort in emotional pain, feeling loved inside, fuel for being assertive and being sustained through life, information for solving problems, and structure for growth? What are you modeling about these value aspects of relationship?

  — With which of your kids, if any, will you need to say, "Sounds like you're having trouble, but I will wait to help you until you ask"? How will you respond when the request finally comes?

- *Make Passivity More Painful Than Activity:* Don't let your child be comfortable in a passive role. He risks getting lost in the shuffle.

  — What will you say to let your child know that you prefer active mistakes to passivity?

  — A child who tries to set the table and spills everything nevertheless receives praise and rewards. When he avoids the task, he loses dessert that night. What will you do to make passivity more painful than activity for your child? Set up some consequences for situations in which you can expect him to be more passive than you want him to be.

- *Allow Time for the Process to Develop:* Kids who struggle with passivity have spent much of their lives fearing and avoiding risk, failure, and pain. So don't expect your child to be a problem-solving dynamo overnight.

  — What will you do to reward little moves this week?

  — And what little moves can you be on the lookout for?

Generally there comes a point when, if the process is working right, the child's assertive parts will become more integrated. Like an engine winding up, your child's activity level will increase. But his first steps will probably be halting ones. Your role is to "encourage the timid, help the weak, be patient . . ." (1 Thessalonians 5:14).

Conclusion (page 190)

Your child needs you to be the loving, limiting, provoking agent who teases out his active parts.

- Your child will resist you and be angry with you as you love him by limiting him and provoking his active parts. How will you deal with that resistance? How do you want to respond to that anger? Remember: Empathize but hold the limits.

Just as the mother bird knows when to push the baby bird out of the nest, use your experience, judgment, and the help of God and others to help your child take initiative to own his life.

In the next chapter, dealing with the Law of Exposure, you will learn how to help your children to be direct and clear with their boundaries rather than falling prey to gossiping and playing parents off each other.

Chapter 13

Honesty Is the Best Policy

The Law of Exposure

I (Dr. Cloud) can still remember what happened that day when I was eight years old. I led my father into the den, not knowing that my sister Sharon and her friend were still in there. I was caught. Here he was, asking me about the broken light, and there they were, watching me seal my fate as a tattletale. On that day I understood the reality: *When you go behind someone's back, you can expect trouble in the relationship.*

- One of the most important principles in relationship is direct communication and full disclosure of whatever is going on in the relationship.

    — When have you learned something about the destructiveness of indirect communication? Be specific about the lesson.

    — When has being indirect in your communication

    Shown you to be foolish?

    Made you a part of the problem?

Made you accountable for the existence of the problem?

Or caused you to get caught up in the devil's snare as you tried to bury anger and strife?

- The Bible says much about indirect communication of truth and the restorative value of direct communication. Direct communication is the best way to go through life.

  — Many people do not communicate directly. Instead, they practice avoidance (ignoring the person or the problem) or triangulation (bringing in a third person) or overlooking. What motivates people to choose these options? Which of these three, if any, have you been most likely to choose?

  — The Law of Exposure says that life is better lived in the light—that is, things are better out in the open even if these things are negative. When have you seen (in your experience or another person's) either a relationship broken by conflict or hard feelings restored by honest communication? Why do you think direct communication works?

Open communication does not mean that we need to bring up every slight or everything that bothers us. But where values are violated or someone is injured or behaving unacceptably, then overlooking, avoiding, or triangulating causes more problems in a relationship. Let's look at some principles that will help your children to be open and honest in their relationships.

Rule #1: Live the Law of Exposure Yourself (page 195)

The way parents communicate both with each other and with their children is the starting point for the Law of Exposure.

- Remember my colleague's wife and their son's reaction to "one of her moods"? She would not ask people directly for what she wanted, and she would not tell them what they had done wrong.

  — What harm can such lack of communication cause?

  — Consider what you are modeling in your home. Do you ask people, especially your spouse, for what you want? Do you tell people what they have done wrong or what they have done to irritate you? What—good or bad—are you teaching your kids by your behavior?

  — What current conflict with your spouse or your children do you need to communicate about directly?

Live out what you want your children to learn. When you are upset or have a conflict with them, go to them and tell them—lovingly, but honestly and directly.

Rule #2: Make the Boundaries Clear (page 196)

A child cannot develop a structured personality in a home where the rules and expectations are not clearly defined. When you have expectations and rules for your children, make sure they know them. This will give you opportunities for "training moments," which occur when both parents and children do their jobs.

- The parent's job is to make the rule. The child's job is to break the rule. The parent then corrects and disciplines. The child breaks the rule again, and the parent manages the consequences and empathy that then turn the rule into reality and internal structure for the child.

— Were the rules clear in the home where you grew up? What did your parents do to make sure you understood what the rules were—and perhaps even the consequences of breaking them?

— What rules in your home today would you like to see become part of your children's internal structure? List your top five. What are you doing to make sure your children know these rules? Are these boundaries clear to your children? If you're not sure, ask them!

Training can't occur if the rule is not clear. Make sure your children know what to do wrong so you can teach them how to do right.

Rule #3: Cure Their Fears and Make Communication Safe (page 196)

The basic reason we do not communicate directly is that we fear the loss of love and we fear reprisal. We fear that if we are honest with our anger or our hurt, the other person will either withdraw from us or be angry. In addition, children think that their anger is much more powerful than it really is. As a parent, you can either cure this universal sickness in your child or reinforce it.

• Review the chart on pages 198–99.

— What is your typical response to the following situations? Choose your answer from either column.

Your child is angry at a limit.

Your child is upset with something you did wrong to her.

Your child is hurt by life.

— What do your answers show you about yourself? Are you pulling away from your child, or staying connected? Are you therefore reinforcing her fears, or curing them?

• Now look again at the key principles guiding those behaviors that cure children's fears (see pages 197, 200).

— Which of these principles would have made your childhood easier?

— Which of these principles, not yet in place, do you need to keep in mind as additional support for your parenting skills?

The main guiding principle for curing your children's fears and making communication safe is this: *Our relationship is bigger than this conflict, feeling, or experience. Our connection and affection will remain after this conflict is past.*

Rule #4: Don't Reinforce Non-Expression (page 200)

There followed an intense exchange when I would not let Susie hide, but that day a bridge was built between me and her blocked-off inner world. Even more important, she had experienced being required to be honest and direct about her experience instead of passively acting it out and wishing for someone to rescue her.

• Generally, withdrawn and defiant children are afraid. Staying soft and loving, while not giving in to their non-expression, will let them know that you are on the side of their fear and pain, but not on the side of their way of handling it.

— When and to what degree is non-expression an issue with your child? Is "Use your words" effective?

— You may have to be more active about pursuing your child's feelings. Interpreting the silence or asking questions helps: "It seems like you are mad [or sad] right now"; "I think you might be upset with me." What can you do to show affection even as you require communication?

— Does your child ever communicate with actions, such as tantrums, yelling, name calling, and running away? What will you do to disallow this form of expression and encourage verbal communication?

A child's behavior will not change in a day. Remember the two ingredients that can help her make that change: showing affection and requiring verbal communication.

Rule #5: Don't Get in the Middle (page 201)

Triangulation is putting someone else in the middle instead of dealing with the person with whom we have a problem. Don't let your children put you in the middle between him and a sibling or him and your spouse.

- In general, except when the situation is unsafe, children need to work out their own conflicts.

  — When have your children seen you work out a conflict without putting someone else in the middle?

— What will you say the next time one of your children tattles on another, trying to put you in the middle? What might you need to do to keep the conflict between them so they learn the necessary conflict resolution skills?

— This same principle applies to the other parent, to friends, and even to other authorities in your child's life. In what current or recurring situation will you have the opportunity to encourage your child to work out a conflict on her own? What will you do to empathize yet stay out of the middle?

Talking with your kids about conflict resolution is great, but requiring them to do it is important even for their problems with school and other authorities. If Mom and Dad are always there to step in with authorities and "fix" it, the child will be lost when her first employer is upset with her performance.

Rule #6: Teach Them Boundary Words to Use (page 202)

We have difficulty knowing what to say when we have conflict with others. We learn what to say over time, but it is a good idea to teach your children what to say and even role-play how they will say things to others when they need to set limits.

• Look again at the list of tools for your kids (pages 202–3).

— What boundary words do you use? When, for instance, have your children seen you simply say no to a request?

— Which one or two statements listed might your child find especially helpful right now? What role-plays will you offer to give your child practice saying—and hearing himself say—these important boundary words?

Your children are dealing with peer pressure, hurtful kids, and strong personalities on the playground. If they are prepared, they will fare better. Role-play with them to give them practice, or find some setting or group for them that does this kind of reinforcing of boundaries.

Bring It to Relationship (page 203)

The ultimate boundary is love. Our connection with each other and with God is the fabric that holds life together. The truth we live and communicate gives this connection and love its structure.

- Everything is ultimately about relationship.

    — As Jesus said, all of the "boundaries" in the world can be summed up in these two laws: "Love God" and "Love your neighbor as yourself." Explain how the use of boundary words is one way of loving your neighbor as yourself.

    — Relationship heals, comforts, and structures our experience. To whom do you turn for healing, comfort, and structure? Why? What does that person offer?

    — What relationships have helped you learn that the love we need is bigger than what we are feeling? What made those relationships helpful?

    — What are you doing to be the kind of person to whom your children can take their feelings, fears, thoughts, desires, and experiences?

As you work on being the kind of person to whom your children can take their feelings, fears, thoughts, desires, and experiences, require them to do just that. And they will be much less afraid of both their experiences and love itself.

Part 3

Implementing Boundaries with Kids

Chapter 14

Roll Up Your Sleeves

The Six Steps of Implementing Boundaries With Your Kid

Whether you are a parent, relative, teacher, or friend of children, we hope you have gained some understanding about the importance of helping children develop their own boundaries and respect the boundaries of others. Concern and insight aren't enough, however. If you put this book on a coffee table or under your child's pillow, it won't do him a lot of good. It is time to get to work.

- In this chapter you learn six steps of boundary implementation with your child. But this knowledge is useless if you aren't setting boundaries yourself.

  — What are you modeling about boundaries for your children? Support your answer with specific examples of your strengths and weaknesses.

  — Your children need a parent who will *be* boundaries. This means that in whatever situation arises, you will respond to your child with empathy, firmness, freedom, and consequences. Define each of these elements and remind yourself why each is crucial.

— Remember, you aren't establishing a partnership with a peer. You're getting ready for battle with someone who isn't at all interested in cooperating with you. So now remind yourself why you are choosing the battle.

Boundaries with kids isn't about "making" your child do anything. It is much more about structuring your child's existence so that he experiences the consequences of his behavior, thus leading him to be more responsible and caring.

Step 1: See the Three Realities (page 208)

You need to come to terms with three realities.

• The first is that *there really is a problem: Your child is not perfect*.

— What evidence do you see of this reality? Be honest with yourself about your child.

— With what aspects of your child's behavior, if any, are you rationalizing genuine problems and playing the semantics game as you describe unacceptable actions and attitudes? Is smarting off "a cute sense of humor," laziness "fatigue," or intrusiveness "high-spiritedness"?

— What honest friend will you consult if you are struggling to see your child's shortcomings?

- The second reality is that *the problem isn't really the problem.* The behavior or attitude driving you crazy isn't the real issue. It is the symptom of another issue, which in many cases is a boundary problem.

  — Look again at the chart on page 209 and the examples of problems that aren't the problem. What, if anything, does this suggest about issues you are dealing with in your home?

  — Consider, too, any crises you have weathered recently. What might the behaviors you've identified suggest about your child? What is your next step in pursuing the root of the problem and helping him to start developing boundaries?

- The third reality is that *time does not heal all.* Time is only a context for healing; it is not the healing process itself.

  — When have you seen that, with nothing but time, things do not improve, but break down further?

  — Infections need more than time; they need antibiotics. What developmental "antibiotics" have you received from this book?

First acknowledge these three realities and then identify and begin to address the problems you see in your child. You will need lots of love, grace, and truth for your child as you get involved in the repair process.

Step 2: Plug In (page 210)

Make sure you connect to good, supportive relationships in addition to your spouse.

- Helping your child with boundaries is exhausting and frustrating work; it can even drive you crazy. You will need much love and help from others.

  — Whom have you found who won't condemn you, who will walk with you through the fire, and who will hold you accountable to do the right thing? When has that person's support helped you stick by your guns with your kids? Give an example.

  — If you don't have such people in your life yet, what will you do about finding or starting a parenting group, a Bible study that works on boundary issues, or a neighborhood group?

Good, supportive relationships offer you a place to trade tips, secrets, techniques, and victories and failures. Parents in denial can come out frustrated, which is what they need. Normal parents come out relieved that they aren't nuts and that there is hope.

Step 3: Grow in Boundaries Personally (page 211)

Before you start preaching boundaries to your child, start walking the walk. Kids are able to sense deception amazingly well. They haven't been on the planet long enough to lie sufficiently to themselves about what they see. They know when you are being a hypocrite or telling them to do something you won't. But even more than that, all of us simply need to be developing and clarifying our boundaries for life anyway.

- Take a look in the mirror from a couple different angles.

  — In general, how well do you maintain healthy boundaries? What are you currently doing to grow in boundaries?

— Review the titles of the ten "Law of . . ." chapters. Which laws do you need to work on the most?

— What, if anything, have your kids said or done that suggests they aren't seeing your boundaries working even though you are wanting them to develop boundaries?

- This step invites you to work not only on your boundaries, but also on your life. You need to be doing the hard work of relating to God and growing spiritually, emotionally, and in good character.

  — It is hard for children to grow when they aren't around growing parents. What are you currently doing to grow spiritually, emotionally, and in good character? What more could you be doing?

  — As you read through the text, did you find that you have a hard time saying no? Or, like the father with the military background, have you realized that you have difficulty respecting others' boundaries? What will you do to remedy any problem you have identified?

If you want your farm to run right, it's wise to ask the one who made the farm how to run it. You need all that God has to help you live. You also need friends who will comfort, support, and confront you on your own weaknesses and selfishness.

Step 4: Evaluate and Plan (page 213)

Evaluate your child's situation and your resources, and develop a plan to deal with the problem.

- **The Child:** Get to know your child's boundary problem in light of who she is. If you haven't done so already, list the following important factors:

  — *Age:* What issues are normal for your child's age group? What is she capable of? At what point are you pushing her beyond her comfort level (a good thing), but not beyond her abilities?

  — *Maturity level:* With regard to attachment, is your child able to connect emotionally to you? Does she see you as someone who cares for her, or is she detached, distant, and chronically cold? When it comes to honesty, does your child tell the truth, or does she struggle with lying and deceit?

  You can also gauge maturity level by considering issues such as

  Basic trust
  Ability to make and keep good friends
  Responsiveness to commands
  Ability to disagree and protest
  Ability to tolerate deprivation
  Ability to accept loss and failure in herself and others
  Attitude toward authority

  Which of these are you concerned about? What events or behavioral patterns have given rise to that concern?

  — *Context:* What is the setting for your child's life? Are you divorced or is your marriage in trouble? Does your child have any clinical issues (neurological, learning disorders, attention deficit disorder)? Are there problems with other siblings? What environmental influences affect her?

— *Specific boundary conflict:* What is the specific boundary issue in your child's life? Is she having problems with family rules, chores, school, or friends? State the issue as simply as possible.

— *Severity:* How profound is the problem you just specified? Be sure that you're not sweating the small stuff. Address issues that involve honesty, responsibility, caring, and morality. Give more latitude within limits to hairstyle, music, and room sloppiness.

- **Your Own Resources:** Now that you are getting a more comprehensive picture of your child's boundary problem, where it comes from, and how severe it is, evaluate what you have at hand to deal with it. Look at the following factors:

  — *Your own issues:* What have you seen about how you react and interact with your child? What causes you to respond inappropriately? What are you doing to grow in that area?

  — *Your life context:* Where, if at all, is there chaos or crisis in your life? What do you need to do to gain enough order and structure so that you can give enough order and structure to your child?

If you are a single parent, where are you finding the help and resources you need to deal with your child's boundary problems? Check with your community, neighborhood, relatives, and friends for assistance.

  — *A boundary-resistant spouse:* Are you dealing with a boundary-resistant spouse? If so, are you—as "pro-boundaries" and therefore mean and depriving—caught in the middle between him or her and your child? What can you do to rearrange things so that the boundaryless parent reaps the consequences of his or her ir-responsibility? See this not as a parenting issue, but as a marriage issue. What are you doing to address the marriage issues caused by boundarylessness?

- ***The Plan:*** Come up with a structure that you will use for yourself and will present to the child. Include the following aspects and write them down:

  — *The problem:* State the problem as specifically as possible. Stay away from char-acter attacks that the child would have to defend herself against.

  — *The expectations:* Make your expectations specific and measurable.

  — *The consequences:* Write what will happen when your child doesn't meet your expectations. Set it up so that, as much as possible, the punishment fits the crime. Set up positive consequences, too, for success in meeting expectations, but don't go overboard in reinforcing anything that isn't savage-level behavior.

Step 5: Present the Plan (page 217)

The more you involve your child in the boundary-setting and boundary-honoring process and the more time, help, and information she gets, the more likely she is to take ownership of it and cooperate in her own growth.

- Invite your child to partner with you even though the plan is still going to be exe-cuted if she refuses.

— Introduce the plan at a peaceful time: What time and place will be good for you and your child? If that moment comes and you're not getting along, wait for another time.

— *Take a "for" stance instead of an "against" stance:* What will you say to communicate that you see a problem that's hurting her and others in her life, that you want to deal with it because you love her, and that you want to work with her?

— *Present the problem:* What specific hurtful effects of the behavior in focus will you talk about?

— *Present the expectations:* What specific standards will you set forth?

— *Present the consequences:* What specific consequences will you establish? Know exactly what your plan is so that you can communicate clearly and directly.

— *Negotiate what is negotiable:* Plan to ask your child for input, within parameters, on the expectations and consequences of your plan. Think ahead: Where can you give a little in those categories? What points are nonnegotiable? What will you say if she asks, "You don't do that, why should I?"

— *Make expectations and consequences easily accessible:* What will you do to remind your child of the expectations and consequences? Where, for instance, could you post them?

You can't control the behavior, but you can control the consequences. Stay in control of what is yours and encourage her freedom to choose. The key is that *if she chooses to resist, the consequences will become a reality*.

Step 6: Follow Through over Time (page 218)

The whole idea of a plan will fall apart if you are not personally functioning as the boundary for the child. This plan all hinges on your doing what you say you will do. Here are some of the things you will need to deal with:

- *Expect disbelief and testing:* Although your child may argue with you when you present the plan, the resistance comes when you are enforcing the consequences.

  — You can expect reactions like shock, disbelief, anger, expressions of hurt and woundedness, isolation, blaming, attempts to pit you against the other parent, and even escalation of the behavior. Which of these do you expect your child to choose?

  — What feelings do you expect to have when your child resists the consequences? What will you do to enforce the consequences? Whom do you have supporting you so you can stay with it?

  — When has a lack of structure and consequences cost you? Or when has being overcontrolled, with no ability to choose, kept you handicapped in making decisions? Let these experiences help you stick to the consequences and not protect your child from reality, from the consequences of her actions.

- *Be patient and allow repeated trials:* Your child is on a learning curve, and learning takes many trials. Expect her not only to transgress the boundary, but also to protest the consequences many times.

  — What will you do to maintain an appropriate level of patience with your child—and with yourself?

  — If you find yourself having trouble with consistently enforcing boundaries, what mature friends could help you explore with you whether the problem is one of resources, abilities, character, or unrealistic expectations?

- *Praise the child's adaptations:* If the process works correctly, you will begin to see less of the bad behavior and more of the good behavior you're after.

  — Why is it important not to focus on your love for your child when you're validating her efforts?

  — What benefits of her new behavior will you help her see? Look for benefits to others as well as benefits to herself.

- *Fine-tune and shift issues:* When you feel the child is mastering the behavior and is more in control of herself, you may want to increase expectations. Or you may want to focus on another problem.

  — What might those increased expectations or that new focus be?

— What will you do to be sure that your child doesn't feel that your whole relationship is about boundaries?

— Your child needs to know that growing up continues all the way through life. What is she seeing in the way you live to reinforce that fact?

We cannot overemphasize how critical it is to stick with the consequences. Remember that every time God disciplines us for our own good, we protest, hate him, whine, shake our fist, and condemn him as being unfair. Yet he loves us enough not to let us call the shots and further ruin ourselves. Your consequence is a team effort by you and God for lovingly nurturing and training your child.

Am I Too Late? (page 220)

An important question parents ask us about implementing boundaries is "Is it ever too late to start?" We say it is never too late to begin doing the right thing for your child and you.

• The younger the child, the easier it is to establish boundaries as normative in life. But children are children, even in the teen years. A child is someone who isn't an adult, meaning someone without the necessary skills and tools to navigate real life.

— Which of the following can you start doing whatever the ages of your kids?

Becoming more honest and more clear about responsibility

Taking more initiative to solve problems

Bringing a sense of structure to your home

Another theme you have found in the text: _____

— Now write out some specific ideas for how to do the task you have chosen to focus on. You may want to refer to the appropriate chapter in the text.

• That smart-alecky, distant kid needs you! Some internal part of your child needs you to get involved and, amidst all his protests, take charge as a parent.

— What specific resources can you bring to bear on your parenting situation? What changes in your life will you make so that you have more *time* for your child? What new *effort* will you bring to your parenting? What *financial resources* will you use for what *program*? What *institutions*—the school, the church, counseling services, and the court system—will you turn to?

— If you're starting to work with your sixteen-year-old, you may have to settle for incomplete results. But why are even incomplete results valuable?

Don't give up on your child, even in the last years of adolescence. You are the only mom or dad they will ever have; no one in the world has the position of influence in their heart that you do.

The Hope You Have (page 222)

Whatever your situation as a parent, God has anticipated it, is fully aware of it, and wants to help you to help your child develop boundaries. He has provided hope for your future and your child's future that is real and helpful.

• This hope comes in the following ways.

— *God Himself:* Review what you know about the God who is the ultimate resource for your parenting, or get to know him by opening your Bible.

— *His Statutes:* What are you doing to learn more about God's principles and laws for developing maturity in his people? Put differently, what plan do you have for consistently reading and studying his Word so that you will gain or strengthen a structure for your life and your parenting?

— *His Reality:* Life works better for us when we do it God's way. Explain why reality is on your side in your parenting. What hope do you find in this fact?

— *His People:* What safe people do you have in your life who can offer you love, structure, support, and guidance? What safe people offer love, structure, support, and guidance to your child?

— *Your Child:* God designed your child with a need to learn to take ownership of his life in submission to him. Your child may not be aware of that need—but you are. What hope do you find in this fact? When, if at all, have you seen signs that your child is learning or even is able to learn what you want to teach him about healthy boundaries?

Remember that you are helping to develop the image of God within your child that is already there and waiting to be strengthened (Genesis 1:27). So use these sources of hope as a help, comfort, and tools as you walk in God's ways and train your child to do the same.

Thanks again for the sacrifices you make daily in parenting, and God bless you.

Embark on a Life-Changing Journey of Personal and Spiritual Growth

DR. HENRY CLOUD

DR. JOHN TOWNSEND

Dr. Henry Cloud and Dr. John Townsend have been bringing hope and healing to millions for over two decades. They have helped people everywhere discover solutions to life's most difficult personal and relational challenges. Their material provides solid, practical answers and offers guidance in the areas of *parenting, singles issues, personal growth,* and *leadership.*

Bring either Dr. Cloud or Dr. Townsend to your church or organization. They are available for:

- Seminars on a wide variety of topics
- Training for small group leaders
- Conferences
- Educational events
- Consulting with your organization

Other opportunities to experience Dr. Cloud and Dr. Townsend:

- Ultimate Leadership workshops—held in Southern California throughout the year
- Small group curriculum
- Seminars via Satellite
- Solutions Audio Club—Solutions is a weekly recorded presentation

For other resources, and for dates of seminars and workshops
by Dr. Cloud and Dr. Townsend, visit:
www.cloudtownsend.com

For other information **Call (800) 676-HOPE (4673)**

Or write to:
Cloud-Townsend Resources
18092 Sky Park South, Suite A
Irvine, CA 92614